My Dears

GW01003416

Ruth with her Mother

Ruth Snary

A Bright Pen Book

British Library Cataloguing Publication Data.
A catalogue record for this book is available from the British Library

ISBN 978-0-7552-1509-6

Authors OnLine Ltd
19 The Cinques
Gamlingay, Sandy
Bedfordshire SG19 3NU
England

This book is also available in e-book format,
details of which are available at www.authorsonline.co.uk

FAMILY TREE

MARY GRACE HOCKLEY b 1908 d 2004
m Percival Ottmann 1936

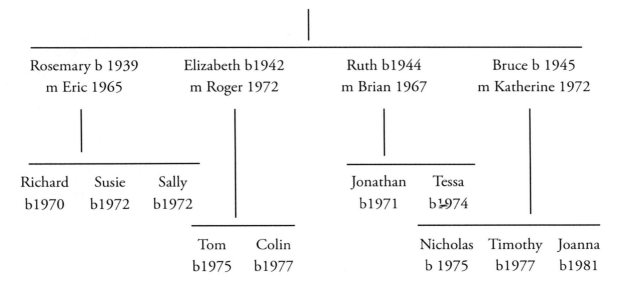

Rosemary b 1939
m Eric 1965

Elizabeth b1942
m Roger 1972

Ruth b1944
m Brian 1967

Bruce b 1945
m Katherine 1972

Richard   Susie   Sally
b1970   b1972   b1972

Jonathan   Tessa
b1971   b1974

Tom   Colin
b1975   b1977

Nicholas   Timothy   Joanna
b 1975   b1977   b1981

Introduction to the letters

My Mother, Grace, adored writing and receiving letters and one of my earliest memories was her joy on receiving a letter full of news from family and friends. She corresponded weekly with her Mother when she left her home in Barry, South Wales, to teach in an East End London primary school. When her four children left home to attend various colleges, she wrote to each of us every week. In the 1970s I began to keep these wonderful letters.

Mother lived near my eldest sister, Rosemary, so there was no reason to correspond with her; my other sister Elizabeth always telephoned her at least once a week as did my brother, Bruce. I wrote to her every week, but also telephoned her quite regularly, and our letters became like a conversation. It was a real pleasure to see her familiar handwriting on the envelopes and then settle down to read the two or three pages of foolscap writing describing her week and referring to my letters to her. She could make the simplest of activities leap from the page with her vivid turn of phrase and her infectious sense of humour.

My sister, Rosemary, once said to me that she was sad that she had not been the recipient of our Mother's lovely letters, and, as the art of letter-writing is seemingly in decline, I decided to collate some of the hundreds of letters that I have kept, and compile them in a book, so that others could share the fun of reading them. Mother did not date her letters, merely writing the day of the week at the top of the page, so that the letters are not in a strict chronological order. The book includes just a selection of the copious number that I have in boxes.

Mother loved reading and sharing her opinions on the latest book that she had read. She could be effusive as well as sometimes vitriolic about a book, but her use of language was superb and it was always a pleasure to discuss a text with her.

The theatre was another love of hers, especially seeing the plays of Shakespeare, whether professional or amateur. She could quote reams of the texts to the amazement of who ever happened to be in earshot. The most surprising events could set her off declaiming. She was a generous but astute critic, often making me laugh out loud when reading her missives.

She loved her church and supported the church in many ways, running a Young Wives group in the fifties, later a Women's Fellowship group, and she also sang in the church choir for many years. She rarely missed going to church on a Sunday and her knowledge of the Bible texts was extensive. She continued going to Bible study classes well into her eighties.

Attending concerts gave her much enjoyment but she felt that her lack of formal musical training meant that she did not fully understand what she was hearing. She really appreciated Eric and Brian, her sons-in-law, giving her guidance when going to concerts.

At Teacher Training College in Wales she had studied botany and calligraphy and after the children had left home she took up her calligraphy pens once again, attended classes, and began a new hobby making greeting cards for family occasions and for friends. Apt quotations were carefully chosen for each recipient and were received with great pleasure.

Mother had such a generous nature and was loved by so many, young and old. Her grandchildren, especially, recall her with great affection as she was always ready to listen with great interest about their exploits.

I hope that you will enjoy the letters as much as I have; re-reading them has brought to life so many memories.

For Lo, the winter is past, the rain is over and gone, Flowers appear on the earth, The time of the singing of birds is come.

A Birthday card for Ruth

Ruth Snary

Grace

As a child, you only know your Grandma for a fraction of your life: perhaps a third. I only knew my grandmother for a quarter of her life because I joined her family in my late teens. I don't remember the day when Grandma started being Grandma because she was the sort of woman for whom beginnings were opportunities for good things coming about: life as a series of small miracles.

Some people spend their life looking for good stories. My grandmother was one of these. For her, the past was something to laugh or marvel at. You never remembered the bad and you often elaborated upon the good. To my grandmother, I was the child her daughter had found at a bus stop looking for a home. Her daughter, Rosemary, scooped me up and took me home, and that was the beginning of everything going right. My grandmother loved to think of things going right, and she has passed that sense of things being right in the world down to her children and their children.

Grandma lived in a world in which things went right even when they were going wrong. She lived by grace: 'grace', meaning a gift freely given by God; a special endowment. Grace is perhaps the ability to find a way through the darkness without worrying where the lights might be: for the person with grace, the lights will always come back on. Grace is a way through things; an order of being that brings one back to life and the living of it. It is the circle of life unbroken and always met. It is a self who chooses to see the beautiful rather than the tawdry. It is a self that keeps moving on, resourcefully.

Grace experienced beauty, compulsively, wherever she was. For her, the world was made up of beautiful shapes and faces: the clouds above her head that resembled galleons or the faces of elves and fairies; or the trees in the churchyard next to her retirement home, 'where I'm going next' she would say, chuckling mischievously.

She saw beauty frequently and commented on it more than anyone else I know. Beauty mattered to her. She saw beauty in the faces of the young children in the congregation of her local church or among her grandchildren. Whenever she didn't see it she was quick to say so, and we laughed, because her sense of what was true was as keen and quick as her senses. If Grandma said you were beautiful, you were; and if she said you were not, then that was also alright. She loved you nonetheless, and you believed her. She was as sure that beauty and goodness existed as she was sure that the current leader of the Women's Fellowship was hopeless at choosing good hymns and organising fun. She noticed things, and she announced what she saw out loud, like a child noticing a large red tractor or a blue whale for the first time. Whatever she saw she said, and even if what she said wasn't what should be said, she said it anyway; and we laughed.

These letters are full of things Grandma noticed and said. She would have liked it very much if I said that her letters remind me of Dickens "Sketches by Boz". So I will say it, because Grandma would approve, and she would laugh at the comparison. Like Dickens's word-sketches, these letters ask for drawings and so they have them; they are like small pencil sketches of her life; notices sent to others of what it is she has seen. They read as a series of moments, of things spotted and then recounted out loud as though to a dear friend.

Grandma was big on looks: how things appeared to her and what appearance might say about character and demeanour. In her letters she notices her grandchildren; her children; the actors on stage at Stratford-upon-Avon and their delivery of her favourite speeches; the language of the books she reads; particularly her beloved Shakespeare, Jane Austen and George Eliot.

Grandma also lived by the sound of words. She listened to sermons in church and the words of Shakespeare spoken out loud on stage whenever she could – a habit from her younger days when she would go to the Old Vic as often as she could, or to Stratford on the bus from Birmingham. She loved theatre and she lived with a sense of the theatrical wherever she was. 'I left no ring with her, what means this lady? Fortune forbid my outside hath not charmed her', she declared to me once, in the role of "Twelfth Night's" Viola, balancing adroitly on one knee in the retirement home in Hove where I had gone to visit her as a surprise. Grandma loved an audience. She also loved the drama of surprises and could always rise to the occasion. Shakespeare often rose with her.

Grandma noticed little things and her letters are full of spotted details of daily things: the look of the washing on the line, the outline of the garden border, the hairdo of the local preacher which wasn't up to much in her opinion. 'What a dreadful haircut' she would whisper (announce) loudly as the terrified woman walked by her to the front of the church. When the BBC cast "Pride and Prejudice's" Jane Bennett as a large, and in Grandma's opinion rather lumpen blonde, Grandma was outraged. Jane Bennett was not supposed to have dopey eyes and frizzy hair. She was not meant to move in such an ungainly fashion. There should be no such things as a plain Jane in Austen. Jane was pretty and graceful. The BBC should know better. Clearly someone hadn't read their Austen.

When a sequel to "Pride and Prejudice" made its way into print, Grandma was again outraged, and she wrote about it in her letters. Nothing could be more offensive than to try and continue the dignified love story of Elizabeth and Darcy through contemporary idioms and gestures. 'Dearest, loveliest Elizabeth' was Grandma's much rehearsed mantra of romantic love. There was nothing to top those adoring superlatives. She loved superlatives and used them frequently. 'I hate it. I hate it' she said of the poor "Pemberley". 'It's ghastly; absolutely dreadful. What utter rubbish'.

'I hate it', 'I love it': Grandma spoke as someone who had a definite idea of what things were worth, especially people. She wasn't afraid to use words such as 'hopeless' or 'fat' when 'fat' simply meant 'bonny and healthy' or something comic, in the case of her stomach. 'It is like a fat football' she used to say, poking her belly and laughing. She loved the absurdity of things and had a comedian's sense of exaggeration. Exaggeration is the beginning of recognising an outline: where to place the emphasis, the outward bulge of the character. She understood that to exaggerate is to make something funny and she was funny. These letters are funny. They are funny outlines of little stories and people. They make me laugh. Grandma's letters often read like a series of pulled funny faces.

Grandma loved stationery, and so her letters are written on nice paper. She had an old fashioned relationship with paper, and she often wrote about the sort of paper she was writing on with real reverence. Paper was important because it was the surface that would carry her written impressions; and those impressions might just stick. Good paper was good manners to your recipient and to yourself as a writer.

Letters have a life of their own, as do people's faces. As such, letters should be lively and tell some news; above all, they should remind loved ones that you are thinking of them. Grandma's letters are bits of news from her corner of the world, and these letters and her phrases, her distinct descriptive voice, still fall out of books I pick up, like leaves from old trees. They are bits of her skin still shedding and they carry with them history: Grandma's but also yours and ours, the years of family history gone by.

We have all lived those years in some form or fashion. Letters fold those years into fragile bits of paper, tucking them away.

When, from time to time, I find one tucked inside the pages of my "Complete Shakespeare" or a novel, I am suddenly hauled back through the sound of her voice to the self I was then. Letters carry the voice of personal history; they carry the sound of personal relationships across the years. As such, they are invaluable proof of our ties to one another, of things shared and experienced years after: vivid moments we would otherwise forget, brought back to us on a sheaf of foolscap paper.

In Grandma's handwriting I can hear her voice, distinct and unwavering, telling me what she thought. Her style is intimate but certain.

As many great letter writers do, she often describes where she is at the time of writing, knowing, instinctively, that this is the best way to share yourself with the person you address. Letters are partly written to share a sense of now, with the understanding that that now can be carried quickly and efficiently, by dint of a stamp, into another home, another life. A letter is instead of a visit or a phone call, but one that keeps. It is a form of intimacy we have largely lost in our culture of rapid movement and accelerated communication. Fortunately these letters have been kept. Fortunately, they can still tell their small, recognisably human stories of family life and years passing; the sustaining love of family life with all of its incidents and accidents, adventures and misadventures, small triumphs and failures and comic moments. These letters are small examples of all the things that go into living ordinary life: things which most of us forget but which we would love to remember – especially as heard through the voice of a loved one.

Sally Bayley

My Dears,

We are stepping briskly into June. I feel I want to catch hold of the months and stop them from going at such a rate. The problems over our porch go on apace as the floods are becoming deeper and more extreme when ever it rains and the builder has been calling about every three months to see if the floods have subsided. He came last week with new ideas to see if they would offer a solution but the rains came and the flood descended, though the porch did not fall down luckily, so he has come again with another idea. Now we await the rains.

The garden has looked a mass of colour with the pansies still in flower, masses of pinks, lots of roses, honeysuckle, iris and the most beautiful yellow snapdragons.

I had a busy day yesterday which started at nine o'clock when the young youth worker from church came for a fifteen minute "Thought for the day" discussion. We are very briefly discussing the Parables of Jesus and he really sets me thinking. Then the builder arrived to tinker with the porch, followed by the gardener who came to cut the grass. Then someone arrived to drive me to the church for the Women's Fellowship meeting and after that I went to a study group in Brighton on David Francis's book "Our Way to God". We meet in one of the old Methodist churches in Brighton which has been modernised. They could have spared nothing, ideas, money, equipment, the lot. I have never seen such a transformation; everything was of the highest quality. The choir, pulpit, pews, gallery are all gone and the most superb replacements, carpeted throughout, beautiful chairs and a lovely wooden glass screen to separate the porch from the church.

I am enjoying reading "The Eminent Victorians" at the moment. I have had the book for years though I do not remember reading it. It is a lovely edition and I relish handling it as well as reading it. Have you read it? I have just finished the Florence Nightingale essay, she was a proper Margaret Thatcher, riding rough shod over everyone to get done what she believed to be needed and right.

It was the Flower Festival at church at the weekend and about fifteen hymns were represented by the arrangements. The hymns ranged from the third to the twentieth centuries and I did the captions for everything. I tried one in Gothic script which I have not attempted before and was pleased with the result. The St Francis Hymn "All Creatures of Our God and King" was represented by a superb life size model of St Francis; on one hand he had a mother bird feeding her young and corn and seed in the other hand. All the flowers were wild flowers beautifully arranged and there was a great branch of a tree and amongst it and the grasses and foliage were birds of all kinds, two nests, one with eggs and another with nestlings. There was a hedgehog, a rabbit, a squirrel, a caterpillar, a bee in a foxglove bell and heaps of butterflies. You had to search for them all. The arranger had made all the animals (like the Lord God!).

The hymn "Eternal Father" had a lifeboat man's jacket, boots and a heavy coil of rope to give meaning to the arrangement of the flowers. The hymn "Glory, Glory, Hallelujah" had a large American flag with an eagle on top and a bugle in the corner; the backcloth was red and all the flowers a vivid red, white and blue. I thought it superb.

Another took up a huge space illustrating "Every Star Can Sing a Carol " and there were stars with the ribbon from each star coming down to signify a different carol, there was a shepherd's crook, a manger, a lamb peeping through the flowers etc, etc. It was a masterpiece.

Now for a good tale. At the Community centre there was an Arts and Crafts "do" and I entered for the Calligraphy (Do you know what that means?) Anyhow, when I went to look there was a red spot on my effort which meant that I was awarded first place but when I looked further I saw that I was the only entry in that section! Oh Well.

Did you know that the Post office often does not frank your letters so your envelope will be used once again. Goody.

Much Love, Mother and Dad

My Dears,

I am feeling very, very dull and stupid this morning. It is Saturday and I miss the sunshine as it is raining. We have been out and fetched the shopping, the milkman has been and been paid, Father has been to pay the paper bill and is now reading about Dennis Thatcher in the Telegraph supplement. He (Dennis) is being regarded as nothing short of a hero and I am quite sure that they are right. Apart from doing a very difficult job he looks something of a Sammy, but that cannot possibly be right as he is a most successful business man. I do not suppose there is anything more difficult for a man than having to play second fiddle to his wife, especially if he is capable and intelligent. I cite the Duke of Edinburgh. As well as the article on Dennis there is a feature about Felicity Kendall and Alan Bates in "Much Ado About Nothing". How I would love to see that but am at the moment itching to read the article.

Yesterday began as a perfect day and we went for a walk up on the (Sussex) Downs but we were caught in an April shower.

"Over the Downs in sunlight clear
Forth we went in the spring of the year:
Plunder of April's gold we sought,
Little of April's anger thought.
(Last lines)
April's anger is swift to fall,
April's wonder is worth it all."
Henry Newbolt

Next Wednesday I am the speaker at the Women's Fellowship but I am not a good speaker and could never give an address so I am going to read lots of bits from the Joyce Grenfell book, telling how her Mother never paid bills and also stories about the royals who, as children went to parties at Joyce Grenfell's aunt, Lady Mary Astor MP, and Joyce Grenfell also attended. It will, I hope, interest them as most of our members were young at that time. I have a photograph that I have had blown up of her writing to her mother, which I will show, and Father has bought me a tape of some of her sketches so I will play a couple, including the very funny "Nursery School" sketch. Joyce's American Mother was the youngest of eleven beautiful and brilliant children and was therefore rather spoilt. She was a wild flirt and reckless with money. When one of the older sisters came to England and married the wealthy Lord Astor, Joyce's grandfather sent her mother to England hoping she would do likewise and marry well. Much to his disgust she married an impecunious architect. Her flirtatious ways and her hopeless money problems led to the marriage breaking up when Joyce was about twenty which was a terrible sorrow for Joyce. Her Mother then returned to the States and Joyce wrote to her every week. She also kept a close relationship with her Father.

Letters mean so much and are a wonderful way of keeping relationships alive.

Much love to you all,
Mother and Dad

My Dears,

Such a lovely and unexpected letter
yesterday, many thanks. My writing,
as I am sure you have noticed,
is much more legible that usual.
This is because my hand will only
propel the biro at a snail's pace. This
blessed 'flu, has knocked me for six
and the doctor said that it could be
a few weeks before I get my energy
back. I was slumped on the sofa and
Father shut himself in the kitchen,
complete with striped apron and
did not leave it until there was no
sign that a meal had been prepared,
eaten and cleared away. Marvellous.

a snail's pace

That book (Margaret Forster's biography of Elizabeth Barratt-Browning) What a book.
An amazing biography- the best I have ever read. I'm glad that I did not borrow yours,
it's the sort of book that enhances any bookshelf as well as the readers mind. EBB was
unbelievably selfish and such an utter fool over her son as well as over many other things,
but I suppose that she was a good poet of her time and there was the most extraordinary
relationship between her and Robert Browning- a sort of "out of this world" feeling
which overshadowed any problems or emotions. I know little of their work, I know "The
Year's at the Spring" come to that, I believe that the "Pied Piper" is his and there are other
familiar bits. I thought that I had his poems but on browsing the bookshelves I found that
I had Mrs. Browning's poems. Her much heralded "Aurora" was three or four hundred
pages long and took half the book, the first poem was a fragment and ran to five pages
and others were great long slushy and sentimental Victorian tales. I was interested to read
the sonnets and most seemed very readable. I don't think that I could face "Aurora."

At the moment, well not exactly at the moment as I am writing to you, but "at this period of time" or as in my other favourite expression "in this day and age" I am reading the History of The Judd School (where Tom and Colin went to school) written by the deputy head for the school's centenary. It is an enjoyable read.

The poetry anthology that you gave me is ideal for convalesance, I sampled the deputy director of the Bank of England's choice and he quoted from something I knew and liked. This is one of the pleasures of an anthology, you come across old loves next to something new. Celia Johnson gave that very funny account of Noah building the Ark and giving God various reasons why it was not completed on time - strikes, late deliveries, shortages of this and that. It's really funny.

Last night I went unexpectedly to see "A Midsunner Night's Dream" at the Community Centre. There are two amateur companies that play there and we have always supported one group which is undoubtedly the better one. Probably the other one has been established longer, it certainly appeared so judging by the age of the performers. As you know (or you probably don't) the play opens with the lines "Now, fair Hipollyta, our nuptial hour draws on apace" and both Theseus and

Hipollyta looked as if they had been married at least forty years and she was a poor actress to boot, he could act but looked so OLD. Then when Lysander appeared with his Hermia my heart sank; both looked well in their forties. The man was good-looking but though he looked too old for the part he and Demetrius were very good. The two women were both over forty and looked it and I longed

to see younger women in the roles. I have seen the actress who played Helena before and never cared for her and besides she is putting on weight! Puck was a charming, graceful word-perfect child, a girl, and if you like a fairy-like Puck, couldn't have been better. I like a male, graceful and rather spiteful but that is neither here nor there, the child was excellent. One of the fairies was a young charming boy but at the end when "through the house give glimmering light" the battery of his torch must have given out and he and Mustardseed had a fit of the giggles! The clowns were not very good, their fustian clothes were hopeless. Thisbe had short hair neatly parted, a white M & S clean shirt and ordinary trousers- he was much improved when dressed as Thisbe. The donkey's head was ridiculous and Oberon's and Titania's outfits matched the donkey's head, dull, colourless and drab. Still I enjoyed the outing and as I know the play almost by heart, hearing was no problem.

I am writing this on my knee so please forgive the ghastly scribble.

All My love,
Mother and Dad

My dears,

Our last letter crossed so I will see what this one can do. It is Tuesday morning and I have half an hour before we have to collect and deliver the 'Meals on Wheels' so I will not attempt to catch the post. There will be two deliveries before I finish it so there might be a letter from you, on the other hand there might not!

I have been making cards. Our art club had its annual show but as I have done no painting at all this year I could not 'hang' any works of art. They had a craft table so I decided to make some cards as I have done quite a lot of writing one way or another. I have been practising the beautiful gothic script which is so attractive when written with a wide nib, so I wrote various names like Heather and Rosemary and painted the appropriate flowers. I did eight for the art club and Dad said that I must charge fifty pence a card at least, so I did. Seven were sold the first day, somebody bought three. Fancy one pound fifty for three cards.

I have just thought about Psalm 121 and the various translations. 'I will lift up mine eyes unto the hills, from whence cometh my help.' The St James version is easily the most beautiful, I never want to read them in the modern translation. The New Modern English translation which I do not like and never use is ' If I lift up my eyes to the hills, where I shall I find help' and the 'Living Bible' which is a marvellous translation but not for the psalms 'Shall I look to the mountain gods for help? No! My help is from Jehovah who made the mountains'

I completely forgot that I had six people coming for dinner on Friday and had arranged for the decorators to paint the kitchen. How I am going to prepare the meal I have yet to discover. The decorators are two women who gave the Women's Fellowship a super talk a little while ago. One is a pianist of no mean ability and the other has a beautiful soprano voice. They taught at a secondary school and for some reason have given it up and have gone free-lance in almost any branch of art or craft that you can imagine. When I saw in their brochure that it included interior decorating I asked them to come and do our kitchen. Dad has plenty to do in the garden. They are a couple in their fifties and they will garden, give concerts, make marmalade or knit, plus anything else that you can imagine. They will finish the painting today and with a bit of luck the bit of wall papering in time to give me an hour to get the meal ready for tomorrow.

Now I must get everyone a cup of tea. Rosemary has kindly invited us to supper this evening as we are all going to Richard's school to see a musical.

Much love, Mother and Dad

My Dears,

Thank you for your willingness to put us all up last week. We all appreciated it greatly and it gave us a rest on the long journey and much happiness. Dad loved the curry and so it appeared did everyone else but I am too old to change my dull eating habits. I liked the various additions to your home, the bathroom curtains, the stool in the kitchen and the new kettle.

On the way home we visited Castle Combe. There are, I think, three roads that lead to it from the main road and we went down the first one and came out along the last one which landed us quite near Chippenham and near the village of Ford. It truly is the most perfect village nothing has been built there for over a hundred years so that you do not walk to the end of the village and come to a housing estate. The village stops suddenly at both ends so you are straightway in the country. Perfect. We went on through Marlborough and picnicked in Savernake Forest.

We were promised another lovely, golden sunny day today but instead it is cloudy and still, not my idea of a good wash day. I have eleven large white tablecloths from our harvest supper at church to wash, I did five last week and the rest today but they are just hanging there limply, refusing to dry, however I would far rather wash the cloths than cook the food.

"Who has seen the wind
Neither you nor I
But when the sheets hang trembling
The wind is passing by".

We have had some glorious days, really warm in the garden and we have done quite a bit of clearing and planting, wall-flowers and sweet william to name a couple of the plants.

Wasn't the Grand Hotel bomb a terrible thing? You can hardly believe that men could plan to kill the whole Cabinet. How can they be so evil, but it is just as wicked when they kill ordinary people in Northern Ireland as they do. The world seems to have gone mad, the Devil must be rubbing his hands with glee, but he will lose in the end. The love of God and man is far stronger than Satan, though at times he seems to have the whip hand.

Yesterday a brother and sister appeared at church for the first time, aged about seven and nine. The lesson was about 'sharing' and each child at church was asked to say what they wanted Jesus to help them share. Most said sweets and such like but the little girl said 'to share my happiness' and when it the boys turn he said 'to share my home'. Lovely. The church is a completely different place from when I came thirteen years ago. Then it was a silent, rather stuffy, immovable group of elderly people, now, bit by bit, it has changed to a thriving vital church with plenty of Mums and Dads and children. It is a modern building with space for clubs, play groups and diverse activities and is much used.

Lots and lots of love, Mother and Dad

My Dears,

This letter is long overdue, but I have been reading the books that you lent me instead of writing. I'm on the last one, the great Trollope tome of over one thousand pages.

The print is quite small, I can't think why he wrote such long novels though I am enjoying it. Emily, the heroine, if you can call her that, makes me mad. As I believe, Ruth, that you read the book some time ago you possibly will not remember much about it. She married Hugh. He was wealthy and she was not and after two years they quarrelled about some words that had been spoken. She makes me cross because she rides such a high horse and he annoys me because he says she must toe his line –Oh! But they love each other – how they love each other!!! He sells up and sends her and the babe to Devon and he stays in London. I suppose I am a quarter-way through the book and glancing at the following chapter heading I do not think that there is time for a reconciliation! I enjoyed "The Little Otterlys" though he was a complete fathead and she unbelievably tolerant and longsuffering. I also enjoyed Trollope's "Vicar Of Bulhampton" a really good tale and if there hadn't been so much crying in Elizabeth Gaskell's "Ruth" and if parts hadn't been so slushy I'd have enjoyed it much more.

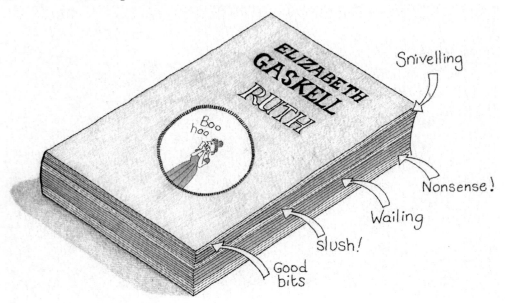

Yesterday I went out to tea to two maiden sisters who live in a bungalow not far from us. One gave a talk to the Women's Fellowship on "Children's Books" and she had perhaps fifty books on display, some, I imagine quite old and valuable, but the talk was hopeless. She would pick up a book to show us and then say "Oh, not that one" and then pick up another and leaf through it to find something to say about it. Then she started to cough, so we gave her a glass of water and then she said her legs were aching so had to sit down!!!! Anyhow they made me most welcome and had lit a coal-fire in the sitting room and made scones whilst I was there so that they would be hot and fresh. I arrived at three o'clock and stayed until seven o'clock because the amazing thing was that they must have had four or five thousand books. One smallish room was just books from floor to ceiling, nothing else in the room. In the sitting room were hundreds more and the shelves in the bedroom were groaning under the weight. I have never seen anything like it. Books on every conceivable subject and by every writer that you could think of, many were very old and must have been of considerable value. It was a fascinating visit.

Time for the post so much love,
Mother and Dad

My Dears,

We got up an hour early too soon. Dad told me that it was seven-fifteen though my clock said six-fifteen. I couldn't hear it ticking, though that is not the fault of the clock, so I got up, made tea, dressed and we were having breakfast by seven o'clock. It is now nine o'clock and I haven't achieved much, just written one letter to thank the Methodist Church at East Molesey for giving the Women's Fellowship such a superb tea last week when we had our coach outing to Hampton Court. We enjoyed the day as it was perfect weather. Dad and I sat on a wall by the river and ate our lunch and then went into the Palace as I wanted to see the Royal apartments. At East Molesey where we were given tea by the church members, one of our members was sitting on a wall when she fell backwards. An ambulance was called and she was taken to hospital and found to have a good lump on the back of her head and painful ribs, so we were telephoned and told that she would be x-rayed and that would be at least half an hour. We had finished our tea but the coach driver said that he did not mind waiting. Our church organist had come on the outing so we all went into the church and he gave us an organ recital! How we were to get the casualty to us I could not imagine but once again our kind coach driver had the answer and drove the coach, loaded with us all, to the hospital a couple of miles away, into the grounds and right up to the door where our member was waiting and we all went home together.

Dicken's "Bleak House" has just been on the box and I thought it very bleak indeed. I had read it a couple of years ago so should have been able to follow it, but half the time I didn't know who was who when I could discern them through the mist. We saw every episode hoping that we would be seeing more than a series of shadowy faces staring out of the screen and saying nothing. Esther gave me the pip though I liked Jarndyce. It's a lovely character and the actor gave a most sympathetic performance. Guppy's acting was first class but the character and performance of Skimpole gave me the creeps. The everlasting sea mist and dim photography was not my cup of tea at all even though it had excellent crits. It was so bitty and so much was left out that it was hard to follow and it left me bitterly disappointed because I was looking forward to the screening.

I feel bone-idle some days but on Monday, when it rained most of the day, Dad and I spring cleaned the sideboard. The green baize in the cutlery drawer was very ragged and shabby so we decided to reline it. We measured up and went to buy the one and a half yards. The woman in the shop thought that we were mad to buy one and a half yards to line a drawer. She said "Do you know that it costs one pound a foot?" So we came home a measured up again and we still needed four foot. So the lining cost us four pounds but it made a good job and the drawer looks spanking. Hope it lasts as long as the other, forty nine years!!

Last week I put two eggs on to boil for a salad and put the hotplate on full to bring them to the boil and said to myself "Don't forget them" and then went into the dining room to write a letter. Three quarters of an hour later went back into the kitchen, you couldn't see across the room, the smell was foul, the thick electric saucepan had MELTED and had a hole in the bottom and the liquid aluminium was in a pool in the drip tray. I switched off, took the saucepan off the glowing hot  plate and as the saucepan was out of shape the lid fell off onto the floor and burnt two holes in the vinyl. I couldn't have done a better job if I had tried!! Hopefully the insurance may contribute something towards rectifying things.

It is now the afternoon and Dad has gone to tidy a neighbour's garden, we had a thunderstorm yesterday and all the gardens look so fresh. I am reading " Lark Rise to Candleford" which is a delightful book. I have had it on the shelves for years and have been meaning to read it. It is a pity that I have waited all this time before delving into it.

Much love to you all,
Mother and Dad

My Dear Tessa,

Well! Well! Well! I looked carefully at your letter and said to myself "I wonder who this is from! I suppose Jonathan has written for some reason", and yet it wasn't a bit like Jonathan's writing. It never dawned on me that this beautifully-written long letter was from you. I read quite a bit before I thought " Good gracious, it's from Tessa" I really couldn't believe my eyes- the writing was so even and attractive that the change from what you used to do was amazing. Your old writing had letters slanting this way and that way, some jumping up in the air, some lying flat on their faces, some curled up and some as straight as a telegraph pole, in fact every variety of position it was possible to do! This was a beautiful letter and such a lovely surprise.

Was your choir concert a success? I expect it was and that you enjoyed the Llangollen trip. Can you say Llangollen (You have to spit or waggle your tongue twice).
Lots of love to you and Jonathan, Mummy and Daddy,

Grandma and Grandpa
To Tessa aged 10

Dear "Grandma"
Thankyou for sending me the lovely box of paints for my birthday love from Tessa

My Dears,

I am sorry to have been so slow in writing to you, I do not seem to have had a minute since returning from holiday but we had a very good and interesting time in Wales and Ireland. Some of the long journeys were tiring, one in particular was hot and wearisome but Frank, the driver, drove us into some glorious woods to a log-cabin camping place. It was a beautiful day and a superb setting and the warden made us all a refreshing cup of tea which was like nectar. We all drank it sitting at tables out of doors and we returned to the coach quite refreshed-it was remarkable. We spent a couple of hours in St. David's and visited the Cathedral; I remembered having a camping holiday there when I was young and then we crossed to Ireland from Fishguard to Rosslare. The first stop was in Wexford, a poor shabby town, and the driver had his wallet stolen but the hotel was good. Then to another dirty town but they had the glass works of Waterford there which was really interesting and we were able to see the whole of the glass-making process. It was fascinating that no seconds are allowed, anything with the slightest flaw is destroyed and the glass re-melted. Even in the poor areas the countryside was dotted with superb, expensive bungalows, miles apart and so isolated that it seemed odd so near the poverty areas. After Cork the scenery and the towns were much improved, through Macroon and Kilkenny. We saw the mountain range Macgillycuddy's Reeks, a name I remembered well from my schooldays. We walked by the Shannon and were driven up high mountains along hairpin bends with perpendicular drops on one side (Ugh). We returned through Limerick, Tipperary (get your atlas out), Kilkenny to Rosslare and had a very choppy crossing as there was a good old wind blowing. We came back through the Welsh Mountains and I felt that they were much more beautiful than the ones in Ireland, but maybe I am biased.

I have taken down the hanging baskets as I couldn't bear to see their bottoms (bare). We must take them to be replanted so that they cover their modesty.

It is such a perfect day I am going to continue this letter in the garden. The new chairs are already in place under the apple tree ready to be sat on so I will see if I can write legibly on my knee.

We have had our final Bible study at the manse for the season and there were nineteen of us there, so we spread out all over the hall and sitting room. We were studying the feeding of the five thousand and one of our number told us that when he was a young officer in the Boys' Brigade they held a camp at Glynde and when they came to the end of the week there was no bread to feed the boys. Another leader suggested that they should pray about the problem and afterwards said that they should go to see the local baker. Off they went and told the baker who said "Leave it to me" and enough bread was delivered to the camp and there were more than twelve baskets left over.

Now I must stop to catch the post.

Much love,
Mother and Dad

My Dears,

The holiday was one of the most successful that we have had. We took three days to drive to the Isle of Mull and three days back so the travelling was too not wearisome, the coach stopped for elevenses and tea breaks. The longest drive was from Brighton to the centre at Scatchwood, north of London. We must have had a relief driver on the coach as he was a Portsmouth man who did not know Sussex. We had five pick-ups in Sussex and as he did not know the way kept getting lost, so it put a good hour on that part of the journey. We then had to drive through London on a busy Saturday morning. When we arrived at Scratchwood where ALL tours start, our coach had left, so a relief coach took us and a good many others going to various places up North to catch up with our coach! We arrived at our hotel in Manchester and realized that we were very near Bruce, so rang him and in ten minutes the whole family arrived at the hotel for half an hour. What a lovely start to the holiday. Our next stop was north of Glasgow and to reach it we drove through Glasgow, a terrible, terrible city, we saw no beauty of any kind, masses of dark grey, dingy, multi-storey blocks and rows and rows of even darker, grey, ghastly dwellings and plenty of derelict industrial sites, a most tragic and pitiful scene and it made one sad to think of people living in such conditions. Even further out of Glasgow the houses were ugly too.

Before reaching Mull we stopped at Inverary for lunch and then at Oban, where we caught the ferry to Mull (the coach went on the ferry too). The hotel, the only one on Mull, had every bedroom facing the sea, the coast of the mainland and the little islands scattered about. We have seen plenty of wild life, seals, deer, herons, oyster-catchers, eagles and of course the views are magnificent, the countryside so quiet and peaceful with hardly any traffic, we would drive for miles on Mull and not see a car. Sheep and the tiniest, snow-white lambs are in every field.

I bought a kilt and a blouse to wear with my navy jacket. When I saw Richard he asked, intending to be funny, if I had bought a kilt and when I said "Yes" he yelled with laughter and surprise. He pictured me doing the highland fling I think!

All the arrangements have been first class and the hotels good, especially the one in Dunfermline on the way home, which was at least ten-star. Everything was new, bathroom tiled from floor to ceiling, great thick snow-white towels and the furnishings really beautiful. All National coach tours from all over the country arrived at Scratchwood within half an hour of each other and then everyone disembarked and looked for the coach which would take them to their final destination. We got to Brighton in record time as the driver knew Sussex inside and out. What fantastic organisation.

Much love, Mother and Dad

My Dears

I seem to have lost count of letters received and letters owing but I think that I have got hold of your last letter, a lovely long interesting one, but with one or two telephone calls, the news, reported and reported on, I am in a confused state so if I repeat what I have said earlier please forgive me.

It is another hot day here, the heat nearly finishes me. I cleaned out the fridge first thing as the freezer bit was solid with ice. I put a bowl of hot water in it and left it awhile. When I opened it a bit later I was able to lift a whole block of ice out in one piece so I put it on the front grass to melt and water the lawn. I had also left my bath water to cool and then carried out a saucepan full at a time to water the front garden but that exhausted me and I spent a spell flat on the settee until a telephone call brought me back to life. I had hoped to get your letter in the twelve o'clock clearance but owing to my prostrate state it was twelve o'clock before I started.

I have finished book two of "The Pallisers" ("Phyneas Finn"). It is a good tale but takes some reading- you haven't read all six have you Ruth? You must have done some skipping if you have. I do not find it easy to skip as I'm afraid that I will miss something important but I managed to miss a bit of the political jargon in book two- Mr. This, Mr. That and Mr. The Other in Parliament but it took me ages to read. As this week has been so hot I have been sitting down and reading for some hours, something I seldom do. I have ignored the crosswords if I couldn't do them easily and read instead. I can still hear my Mother saying when she caught me reading in the day 'Can't you find something better to do Gracie'? She would have been well into her second century now. Before I start book three I want to read 'Othello' again with that horrid, clever Kenneth Tynan's notes at my elbow. I see that "Fortunes of War" is being shown again on the telly so that will mean a second cheque for the actors!

Two letters from have come from Richard at the same time, one took a month and the other two weeks. He was bitten by a sea urchin and it was VERY painful and became swollen. He was yelling with the pain and an American gave him the elegant advice to "piss on it". Eventually he did do and immediately the pain disappeared. Apparently that is the recognised cure, simple and cheap.

Much love, Mother and Dad

My Dears,

I have just about thirty minutes before I go to the hairdresser's and if I leave this letter and finish it when I get home, I will probably miss the post, so it will be short and sweet but it is chiefly to thank you for the book of poems by Ursula Fanthorpe which I find quite delightful. I have read all of part one and many of the others and not one did I find unintelligible though I did read one or two over a second time. I've read the one entitled "Patience Strong" several times and go along with the first part of the poem. I find the second part full of tolerance and understanding which is quite touching. It is like the Women's Fellowship*, they all love Patience Strong and if ever they give me a small gift it is invariably a book of her poems which they are quite sure will give me great pleasure. I never know what to do with the books, but I do believe most sincerely that she does have a real value for a great many people. It is a good thing that we are all not alike as the world would be a very dull place. How far from dull it is, I have only to look at my three lovely daughters and see three people so utterly different and yet so attractive and good to us both and to a great many other people as well, that I am filled with joy and a deep thankfulness. Amen! Thank you again for sending the poems. I shall have a great deal of pleasure from the book. Nancy** once sent me a paperback book of the poems of Ted Hughes and I cannot understand many of them.

I had a lovely and most unexpected gift from the Reverend Rose, a small hardback of the most beautiful prayers collected by Elizabeth Goudge (I've read a couple of her novels and enjoyed them) but these prayers are from all sources, some very ancient, others modern and they are superb.

I have been doing more homework; "Cider with Rosie" with Susie and yesterday "The Tenant at Wildfell Hall" with Richard. We discuss what they have to do and then they get on with it. I love doing this as it refreshes my memory of the books which I then read again at leisure.

I am now a beauty queen as Dad says every time I emerge from the hairdresser's and the sun has come out so it is a beautiful day. We went to Kipling's old home in Rottingdean and sat in the glorious high-walled garden. It has been transformed from a wilderness of long-standing into a haven of beauty. Such Pleasure.

All my love,
Mother and Dad

*Grace was chairman of a Women's Fellowship group at her church for many years
**Nancy, a school friend of Grace's

My Dears

I had planned to write to you this morning and then Dad reminded me that I had promised to visit an old lady so I had to abandon my plans and plunge out into the rain, leap two rivers rushing down Upper Kingston Lane to visit Mrs Pinder. She always tells me about her youth, but she is quite jolly and her life has not been dull so I sit and enjoy it. She talks solidly so that it is a kind of rest cure for me, if I needed one.

Thank you for my Mothering Sunday card. We had a packed church for the service with children making up half of the congregation. Some of the children received an award for making a scrapbook about God's world and others for learning several verses from the Bible. They all received posters of either animals or children, which were rolled up like scrolls and they were told not to unravel them until the end of the service. The line of forty children out in the front of the church seemed like a long, long trail a-winding!

Rosemary was the speaker at our Women's Fellowship last week and everyone enjoyed her talk. She spoke about the Sunday School and she brought some of the equipment that they use and some of the work that the children have done, so it was good. Also, everyone could hear which is more that can be said of some of our speakers. I am giving up organising the Fellowship. Normally the Minister's wife is the Chairman but for the past fourteen years they have not wanted to do it but Margaret is a born leader so I can fade away. I will miss it as I have loved the work but I will be glad to finish.

Bernard Levin's book is absolutely super – each article seems more interesting than the one before. He certainly has a way with him, I AM enjoying it. Thank you very much indeed. Did you notice the design on the cover? I would love to have been good enough to design covers. It was "In THEse TIMES"

I do not suppose that you watched Wogan on Wednesday. I seldom do unless Dad says that someone interesting is on. On Wednesday he interviewed Magnus Magnsson so I watched and of course the conversation turned to Mastermind. M M said that they always had four people in reserve in case any one panicked so he had the four there on Wogan and he put them through their paces. He went though the lot as normal (more or less) and we didn't twig until the end that it was an April Fool! The funniest question was "What novel begins with these words?" and then MM gave a great long sentence in French. I thought that it was so unfair to give such a long quote and take up so much of the two minutes allowed but the contestant said " Would you repeat that please?" and MM did in all seriousness. Another used the most obscure expressions and the longest words I have ever heard and at the end MM awarded the one with the fewest marks the top prize. We fell for the April Fool, hook line and sinker.

I have just watched the Grand National and my horse lost his way completely so it is time for a cup of tea.

The cyclamen that you gave me refuses to lie down, there are still five blooms full of beauty and they have blossomed for SEVEN months. What is amazing is that the leaves are as fresh and dark green as when you bought the plant. I believe that I have pulled off just one leaf but I am not sure about that. It is quite unusual for the leaves not to turn yellow and drop off, so it has certainly done its stuff. We had a white one about the same time and before you could say "Jack Robinson" every leaf had turned yellow and for a short while the plant flowered absolutely leafless so the flowers decided it was rather unpleasant living with not even a fig leaf, so drooped and died themselves.

All my love, Mother and Dad

My Dears

I have been busy with my homework this weekend. Richard and Susie have the same English master. He is the devil for the homework that he sets - what he will give them when it is time for "O" Level I cannot imagine. He demands all that they can give and then some more. I think it is good to stretch them especially when their brains are stretchable. Susie had an essay on "Macbeth" which we plotted out on Sunday afternoon and Richard had one on "Julius Caesar" which I have been re-reading and will go over with him tonight. Last Tuesday I had a go at "The Pilgrim's Progress" for the same master. Richard told me of one boy in this class who does the most fantastic English work and brought me one of his exercise books to read. It was absolutely staggering, I could not believe that it as written by a fifteen years old. Most glorious English, beautifully written with never a mistake. It really was superb work. He will surely be a writer when he is older. You can see by the master's remarks that he is deeply impressed.

I'm off to the hairdresser's in twenty minutes so I cannot write much more. Can you watch "Yes Prime Minister"? It's superb. There was a feature on it in The Observer with a photograph of the cabinet room (the BBC one!) so I have cut it out and put it in my copy of the scripts.

I am re-reading David Cecil's "Portrait of Jane Austen" a most lovely book. When it is finished I am going to read all six of her novels again. I have already read them several times as they suit me. I am very conservative, in fact quite boring in what I read, eat and enjoy and wish I were more of a liberal or even a socialist.

Thanks for the envelope; I haven't got a five pence stamp so this will have to go second class.

Lots of love, Mother and Dad

My Dear Ones,

How I love your letters arriving – I like to savour them before I open them. Many, many thanks for keeping me informed of all that you do. Guess what! Eric has been given two tickets for Britten's "Midsummer Nights Dream" rehearsal at Glyndbourne AND Rosemary is away for the weekend so Eric made a list of the people he could take with the second ticket and, believe it or not, he put his old Mother-in-Law as number one. I was quite touched and thrilled. I've just listened to my recording, all six sides, using my earphones, and tried to remember what you told me, Brian, but I could do with a few more lessons. I haven't forgotten about Snout's half-tones and I am getting used to the music, in fact I love the fairy music and find the clowns' parts very amusing. Titania I also like and a lot of Oberon. I am becoming more tolerant of the lovers, though I cannot say that I really enjoy their music. The one I like least is Theseus (I have John Shirly-Quirk on my recording,) there seems to be no music, melody or sweet sounds in that part at all, but I am longing to see it.

The sun is still shining so that I can hang the towels on the line this afternoon. I have done a pile of washing lately, everything from the little bedroom including the eiderdown and the pink curtains which were so heavy that they nearly finished me. The curtains then finished the washing line which snapped in the middle! Dad had just cut the grass and watered the roses so that the curtains were covered in grass cuttings and mud from the rose bed!!

I am reading "Lorna

WHUMPH

Doone". I read it when I was young, it's quite a remarkable book, a fantastic style and turn of phrase but it's a tome to get through. I have had a couple of sessions before six AM and it is still not finished.

Lots and lots of love to you all,
Mother and Dad

My Dears,

Will the winter never cease? There is a bitter wind here again, and no sun and Dad is on the sick list so we are awaiting the doctor. It is a blow as we were going to London with the retired members of the Electrical Association to visit the Thames flood barrier followed by lunch at the Power Station and finishing with a visit to the Houses of Parliament. I am hoping to be able to go to the Proms to hear "Belshazzar's Feast" with Simon Rattle conducting the Royal Philharmonic Orchestra and The Brighton Festival Chorus. I have their recording with Ben Luxon as Belshazzar. Now Eric has lent me the score so I hope to do some homework before the Prom.

All this before I have thanked you for your ever-welcome letter. It is lovely to hear your news.

I am interested in Storm Jamison's "Company Parade" but it is an odd book. There seems no stability in the lives of the characters, their emotions change from one minute to the next, laughing one moment, crying the next, hating and loving before you can turn the page, but I expect life was pretty unstable and emotionally fragile after the first world war.

The Women's Fellowship secretary has almost completed the programme for next year and I have spoken to Maud Lord (how would you like a name like that!) about taking over from me as Chairman but we must wait until the new minister and his wife arrive before making a decision as she might like to be chairman. The last three minister's wives were only too thankful to be nominal presidents only.

There is a good calligraphy class in Southwick on a Monday evening and the work displayed this week was superb so I would like to try and improve my efforts. Next winter I will see about joining.

Lots of love to all,
Mother and Dad

My Dears,

I have just watched ten minutes of John McEnroe on the Centre Court performing with such ill grace and bad temper that it is no hardship to leave the box and to do something much more pleasant. Many, many thanks for your, most welcome letter with its enclosures. The program of Jonathan's production of "The Frogs" was fascinating. I was amused and charmed to see his name in the programme as Jon as you have always insisted on calling Jonathan - Jonathan and now he has taken the matter into his own hands. Young Tim has just done the opposite and won't answer unless he is addressed as Timothy.

Last Saturday Tom was playing for The Judd School cricket team against Christ's Hospital at Horsham so as it was a perfect day Dad and I went to watch. We got there for two o'clock start but it didn't start till two-thirty! We went into the school grounds and parked the car and then asked one of the boys standing around which way to go and he said he'd take us. We had chairs with us and he carried one and we set off on a country trek. The school has TWELVE pitches. The grounds seemed to stretch for miles; the boy eventually found the pitch where Judds were playing and we parked our chairs and sat in superb surroundings on a glorious afternoon. Then the teams came on and the Judds were fielding. We failed to decide which one was Tom as we were a long way away on the boundary but after the first innings was over they all went to the other boundary for a drink, so took our chairs and went over to find Tom. We then found that we have been looking at the wrong match! Judds had fielded three teams so we made further enquiries, picked up our traps and, with a girl this time, were taken a few miles to some more pitches and found the right match but Judds had batted first and were now fielding so we didn't see Tom's performance at all! But it was a lovely, heavenly day and we did enjoy ourselves.

It is another lovely sunny day here but the garden is sadly in need of water, so Dad is carrying cans of water each evening to help things along.

We are to entertain a foreign student tomorrow and have been given the name, but haven't a clue whether it is a man or a woman! Life is full of surprises.

This is a funny letter, well hardly amusing, but you know what I mean.

Much love, Mother and Dad

My Dears,

Here goes September. It is quite crazy the way the months fly by. I try to enjoy each day as it comes but they still slip through my fingers.

Thank you for the three letters, all most interesting about your French adventures. Yours, Jonathan, of the antics of the bulls was very entertaining and Tessa's quite different but together with yours, dear Ruth, gave a very good idea of your French holiday. The return via the Cathedrals was a really excellent plan as it made the journey purposeful and in consequence must have been less fatiguing.

The wind has brought down hundreds of our apples but there are still a lot left. I believe that fierce winds are forecast for tomorrow so I hope we will be left a few as they are not ripe yet.

Last evening Susie and Rosemary came as Susie wanted a discussion over three of Sylvia Plath's poems. When I knew that it was about modern poetry that she had to write I felt hopeless and helpless but discovered on reading them that they were quite fascinating and not difficult to understand. I really enjoyed having a glimpse into their studies once more as it is months since they asked for my help. About a year ago we did a great deal together which I really enjoyed.

I have just re-read "Tom Jones", a seven hundred pager and am now on "Vanity Fair" for a second reading which is another novel of the same length. "Tom Jones" became a bit tedious but I do not think that I will find "Vanity Fair" so as it is such a good tale. I enjoyed the first episode on the television but half hour once a week is far too slow.

I have also bought some books with the ten pounds that the Women's Fellowship gave me, three George Eliot's "Romola", which is not published in a hardback so had to buy a paperback but the other two, "Felix Holt" and "Scenes from Clerical Life", I was able to buy with hard covers. I also bought a paperback of Jennifer Uglow's (what a name) book on George Eliot's novels. Parts of the first chapter were way beyond me but then she devotes a whole chapter to each novel which is fascinating. The stuff that she and George Eliot had read is amazing, I had never heard of most of it or of the writers, reading it made me feel so ignorant but other parts cheered me up.

Tessa, your poem is on display at the Southwick Library. It is advertising the Calligraphy classes. I can catch the afternoon clearance if I stop now.

Your loving, Mother and Father

My Dears,

A very happy new year to you all, it is still very mild here as I imagine it is everywhere. I did a huge wash yesterday but first I managed to flood the floor of the kitchen. When I had put my new twin-tub machine away after the previous wash I had not switched everything off so that when I ran the tap-water into the tub it was leaving the machine at the same rate out of the emptying tube. I was not aware of this until I found myself paddling in the water which of course had gone every where. I could have sat down in the middle of it all with vexation. But never mind as I had your present to enjoy. How can I express my delight at the book of poems that you gave me? When I was at school we had to buy our own text-books but when I went into

the sixth form the books were provided, the very time when the books we studied, for English at any rate, would have been the ones we would have liked to have kept. One book was a very small volume of "modern" poetry which I loved. I tried to buy a copy some years later but it was out of print. Then I saw a copy amongst Zilla's (a school friend) books and really coveted it but she too liked it, and wanted to keep it. I knew many of the first verses of the poems and several whole poems in the book and many, many times I have wished to read the poems once again. When I opened your parcel I thought at first that it consisted only of modern poems and wondered if I would enjoy them but when I looked into the book there were all the poems of the ones I had loved so much and longed to have copies. I was overjoyed. It is a beautiful book and I keep finding more and more of the poems that I loved. The modern poems do not seem too way out either so it is going to become one of my treasures. Many, many thanks.

I hope that you had a happy day for Jonathan's seventeenth birthday, he sounds just like you on the phone, Brian, the weather at any rate was in festive mood. It has been quite perfect here and the garden is full of crocuses and even some daffodils are out in a few places. We have had hours of sunshine.

Did I tell you that we had front-row seat for Kenneth Branagh's Renaissance Theatre Co. They are doing three Shakespearean plays, "Hamlet", "Much Ado About Nothing" and "As You Like It". I would gladly have seen all three but felt grateful that I was able to see one, "As You Like It". The seats were on a level with the stage as when we booked, there were no other seats available for the whole week so we were lucky to have the front row. It was a packed, marvellous audience and I could hear EVERY word. Oh! It was wonderful to hear like that and see such a superb and amazingly funny production. Branagh was Touchstone and Celia was a scream, utterly delightful though so funny, so different from the sweet and docile character that I have always seen or imagined. The song "It Was a Lover and His Lass" was to a modern tune which I longed to hear over again as it was so funny. You can imagine how the "hey ding a dings" would lend itself to riotous humour. It brought the house down. The whole cast took the curtain calls over and over again, no one was picked out as special; Branagh was somewhere at the back.

It is after lunch so I will address the envelope and get this into the post.

Your loving, Mother And Father

My Dears,

It's blowing a gale and the rain lashed across the back garden and this afternoon the Women's Fellowship went for our outing around Sussex to see the Autumn colours, despite, "Heigh Ho, the Wind and the Rain" (Shakesperare's "Twelth Night") there are NO autumn colours yet awhile; on our way back from Bristol I did see one sumac shrub in someone's garden but I cannot remember where it was so we cannot make a beeline for that! The forecast did say that the afternoon would be less violent so one never knows. We had planned to go to Rottingdean to sit in Kipling's garden but changed our minds in case it was wet or cold and as it is wet AND cold it proved a wise decision. We went on the coach but the trees and hedge-rows were in full leaf, all fresh and green, hardly a sign of autumn anywhere, and to make it more like summer, the rain poured down without ceasing the whole time. The windows of the coach were steamed up and everyone started cleaning the windows to see out, and on looking out the whole of Sussex was under a thick mist with the sky a dense grey. We arrived at Arundel and leapt puddles, forded streams in search of somewhere for tea. We arrived home an hour earlier than planned and all were glad to be home. But we did have some fun and enjoyed the colours of the mackintoshes.

I am well into "Sibyl", I nearly gave up reading the first chapter or so about the nineteenth century Prime Minister and the politicians, which reminded me forcibly of the ghastly history mistress we had for our School Certificate. She was deadly boring and we studied that period which left me hating and ignorant of that period. I survived the chapters and am now well into the story.

Much love to you,
Mother and Father

My Dears

Many thanks for your most welcome letter and this missive comes with our wishes that you have a very happy birthday.

I have been making tabs for our new rose trees as most of the old roses died in the bitter cold. My Hoover was sadly in need of new brushes. I have used it for nigh on hundred years and it literally picked up nothing. Dad rang some firm and the chap came along and took the Hoover away. He brought it back the next day with the bill for fourteen pounds and fifty pence and I did not recognise it; it looked brand new in every respect and it works like a bomb!

The Bernard Levin book delights me more and more. There is a scathing article about the Pre- Raphaelites. Richard had to do some work about that lot and I became involved and learnt a great deal but I would have liked to have read Levin at the time in order to give a completely different point of view. He hadn't a good word to say for them- not even the famous one of the drowned Ophelia by Millais. He said that you could see the rim of the bath tub!!!!!

A new meaning for the term carpet bombing?

I have a copy of his "Speaking Up" but it is a paper back and I remember that he once wrote that a paperback was not really a book and I go along with that as well as most of all else that he writes. I love a hard cover and a beautiful hard cover is a fine possession even if the material inside isn't all that remarkable- a good text is a bonus!

We spent most of last week visiting the sick and aged and we had a famine lunch at the Manse on Thursday and another after church on Sunday. I do not help in these efforts but I often wash the tablecloths afterwards. I did six this week, great huge white things,and I wish they would wear out so that they could be replaced with something more practical.

The Brighton Festival Chorus are singing "Belshazzar's Feast" at the Brighton Festival and the other work is Walton's "Façade" but I find "Façade" difficult to listen to. The words of Sitwell's poems blot out the music for me and yet the words are unintelligible. I have them all in my book of Edith Sitwell's poems but with exception of a few, the rest are complete nonsense, so I am going to obliterate the words from my mind and listen to the music, just remembering the dance rhythms that the music expresses. The words are to be spoken by Eleanor Bron and Robin Ray so I will be interested to see them in the flesh and close up as we have stalls seats.

I gave you ten pounds when I saw you so the enclosed is to buy yourself a flower.

Lots of love and birthday greetings, love to Jonathan and Tess and to dear Brian, Mother and Dad

My Dears,

Many thanks for all the birthday greetings. I had thirty two cards and quite a number were most attractive. One was a picture of San Giorgio in Venice which I will add to my Venetian collection. Fanny, my cousin, wrote that it was her favourite church and that she had sat in it for hours just admiring its proportions. She must be a fan of Palladio. I still have my Mother's Day card on show as I like it very much, together with a delightful card from Liz with a background of the Grand Canal.

Jonathan certainly went to town with his card it must have taken ages to do, please thank him. Tessa, your writing has improved out of all knowledge and I liked the puzzle words on the cover. I solved the puzzles with a bit of help from Susie-thank you all.

I am half way through "Hotel du Lac" and am MAD that I did not see it on the television especially as it was with Anna Massey whom I admire very much, but we were with Bruce so it would not have been very convenient to watch and I did not know about the book until your gift arrived. I do not enjoy TV without my earphones when I can hear perfectly.

The Old Vic was all that I hoped it might be. When I was young in London, I used to go to every production which changed every three weeks. I first sat on the wooden steps in "the gods" for ten pence and then moved up (or rather down) to the pit for one and tuppence where we sat on forms with no backs. I never rose above the one and tuppences. Now the new Canadian owner of the Old Vic has spent two million pounds on it and it is a superb theatre. We had centre-front-row stalls, twelve pounds and fifty pence each, for an adaption of Pride and Prejudice, but it meant that I could hear it all as we were quite close to the cast and it was a superb evening. It got to the essence of the book and the audience (the theatre was packed) was in total sympathy. You felt that they were all Jane Austen fans and were delighted with the production. Tessa Peake-Jones was a charming Elizabeth and Peter Sallis as Mr Bennet was just perfect. Liz saw the same production at the Birmingham Repertory Theatre and loved it.

All my love to you,
Mother and Dad

My Dears,

A super, super parcel. I met the postman and he looked at his letter pile and said "Nothing today" Alas!Alas! Amazingly in a shortwhile he knocked on the door with the parcel that had been in his bag but I never expected such a content, your lovely letter and the book I was longing to possess. Thank you very much indeed. I am loving my foraging into "Elizabeth Gaskell's Life and Works" and am reading it between reading her novels. Her short stories I read in one gulp which was just right, as there is a chapter about them. I have just come to the part in the book where she meets and becomes friends with Charlotte Bronte. I am loving it all, so again thank you.

We had great excitement last weekend as an acquaintance of Father's, Cecil Cambell-White (I recall the name but do not remember seeing him) rang to see if he could call on us arriving on Sunday evening. He is eighty or eighty one. Do you know how he arrived? In a SILVER ROLLS ROYCE!! I could only hope that the neighbours happened to be looking out of their windows at this time! We had no idea how long he was planning to stay but he started talking as soon as he put his foot in the door and did not cease until he left next day! He was very knowledgeable and was interested in everything and anything, but I was worn out with listening. He came over to England from India to prep-school when a child, went on to public school, then a scholarship to some college and into the RAF. He flew into promotion but not in an aeroplane, married a model, divorced her and married a doctor from South America and had four children. He had been driving round France before calling here and brought me a huge bunch of yellow roses. Today I received the most Rolls Royce letter than I have ever received (excepting family letters which are better than all RRes). It was beautifully written, beautifully expressed with tiny writing that covered two sides of notepaper. The visit was a bolt from the blue as we haven't exchanged Christmas cards for over fifty years. It was such a pleasure to see him.

I do not like it when I do not write to you. Telephone calls are very pleasant and I enjoy them, but you can always read a letter a second time to correct everything that you have misheard, got wrong, do not like, have time for second thought etc, etc, etc. I have done my jobs so can sit down with an easy mind and write to you, but oh dear, the hairdresser is coming in fifteen minutes so I will be interrupted!

It is now the afternoon, my hair is in pristine condition, the weekly shop is done, the sun is shining, we have had lunch and a cake is in the oven so that I can return to my letter.

We had a long letter from an old friend who attends the church where we were members in Birmingham. Apparently the choir has been disbanded, but not in the most tactful of ways by the young parson and it has upset everyone's applecart. It is so sad but there must be hundreds of "choirs" all over the country that should have been obliterated years ago and nothing is more difficult to carry out. So many have given such faithful service over many years. In the Birmingham choir, one soprano had been in the choir for over forty years and, as poor as the choir may be, the members still love being part of it.

Rosemary is coming at some point so I will have to stop again but I may be able to catch the post. She had a bit of luck this week. She had left her new glasses on a train so she contacted British Rail and was sent a form to fill in, which she duly did, and returned it with not much hope and amazingly they were returned to her in the case, undamaged. How is that for a spot of honesty?

All my Love, Mother and Dad

My Dears, especially Jonathan,

We both wish you, Jonathan, a most happy birthday even though as Tessa said you will be spending your birthday on a coach. I believe that you have your own bank account but I am not absolutely sure so I wrote the cheque to your father just in case I was mistaken. If you let me know I'll remember in future(with a bit of luck).

Tomorrow we go up to London very early so that we can look after Nick, Tim and Joanna whilst Bruce and Kate go house hunting. I hope that they can are lucky and find a house that suits them.

We have received fifteen pounds from the government for Auntie Flo's funeral expenses. If you were born before a certain date you only get half-fare to heaven and if you were born even earlier you get nothing so maybe have to walk. The first class fare is thirty pounds. Quite crazy.

This page has been written after a lunch of liver, bacon, sausage, onion and mushrooms. This hotel only serves meals on that scale at weekends, Brian, so do not bank on a high-class menu when you come to stay, but we will do our best as we are looking forward to your visit very much. We have a man who sells fish from a van from various pitches in the area which have supposedly jumped straight out of the sea and this week I bought a couple of trout that had swum down the river Adur and they were really delicious. Now how often have I written about food? I cannot recall another occasion.

Your ever loving, Mother and Father

Norman, Hilda and Grace

Grace in her twenties

Grace's Wedding 1936

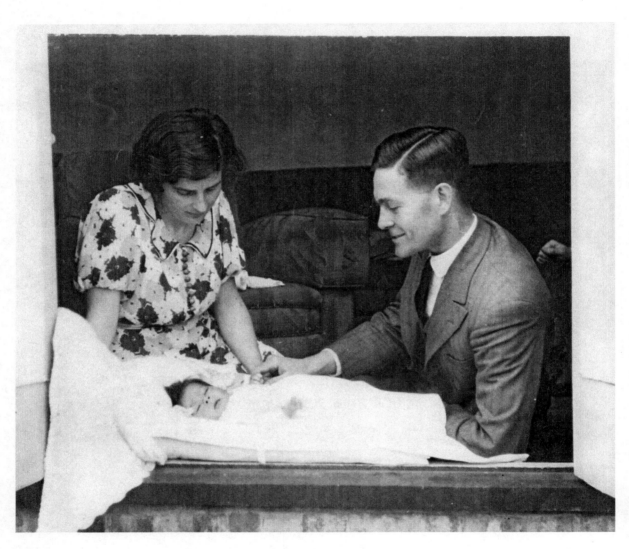

Grace and Percy with Rosemary 1939

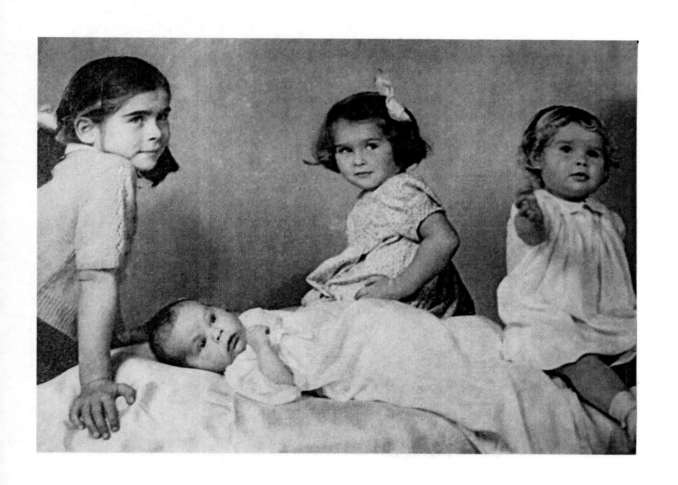

Rosemary, Bruce, Elizabeth, Ruth 1945

Grace and Percy 1967

The Family in the Seventies

My Dears,

If I had a computer and could work it, I would design a beautiful heading for this fine notepaper but I haven't a computer and if I had I wouldn't know which knob to press so you must be content with this unadorned foolscap. However it comes with much love and your letter this morning was just what I needed, required, wanted, hoped for and dreamed about. It has inspired me to put pen to paper, albeit a biro. Thank you very much. Last week

I idled the time away, wasting whole days. The crosswords were bewildering, it must have been a new chap because I couldn't understand what he wanted. Anyhow on Saturday the sun shone, the air lightened around the crossword and I finished it.

What do you think that I have started reading? "War and Peace". It's a vast tome and I doubt if I shall see it through but it is divided into quite small chapters which is an incentive to do a bit each day. I read it ages ago but cannot remember a thing about it! I would like to be at your discussion of Vera Brittan's "A Testimony of Youth" I can hear the actor who played her father on the television saying in his Yorkshire accent "our Vera". I don't feel able to read it again- the war parts are so tragic – all that loss of young life – it would be like losing all my precious grandsons.

The narcissi that you sent are amazing. I planted them in a pot and there were small white bits showing, one lying flat on its face. In two days all had turned green, the lazy one raised its head and is now keeping pace with the others. The tallest, about two foot high, is in full flower and another two, a bit shorter, have fat buds. Many thanks for the present.

That's the lot for today.

Your ever loving,
Mother and Dad

My Dears,

Lovely, lovely it is a marvellous photograph which I am thrilled to have. The humans in front of the most delectable building make a perfect picture, its so good of each man that it makes you feel that you'd probably like them if you knew them and then you realize that you know them very well- just a son-in-law and a grandson.

No word came from Liz last night about Tom's operation and I went to bed, sad that we had not heard but did my best to leave it in God's hands, He who can guide the surgeons hands, support the watchers and heal the sick. I am sure that we will hear soon.

I seem to have made so many cards recently that I was ready for a rest and couldn't make much effort to do anything so I sat down and read "Persuasion". It took Louise two months to recover from a bump on her head and when they went visiting it was normal to go for four to six weeks. They would have been greatly surprised to have been with us when Jonathan drove us at seventy mph to Carmarthen and to see a "Fast food van" overtake us. How different their life was then but it's restful reading about it.

Did I tell you that there was a bomb scare at Susie's college during their exams and another at the local hospital where all the patients had to be evacuated? Isn't it wicked?

CONTENTMENT !

Is your new old fireplace in situ? There is always something new to see at your house- we have two new shiny taps in the kitchen!!

Much Love, Mother and Dad

My Dears,

Thank you for another short-story. Your letters are better than some novels. We had a book sale at our church hall organised by the local library. There were thousands of books and hundreds of buyers – the room was packed so it was a job to get near the books. We bought a few at ten pence each (less than your postage stamp) but nothing startling – a few thrillers to take away on holiday, one by Gavin Lyall who is Katherine Whitehorn's husband. I have often wondered what sort of writer he was and now I will know if I read his book!

I took Dodie Smith's autobiography out of the library and then found that it was part two. The first part must have been about her infancy as this one began in her early teens. She is probably someone that you have never heard of but she was THE playwright (How do you spell the write/right part of that word?) When I was young I sat open mouthed watching her plays "Autumn Crocus" and "Dear Octopus" etc. Well, she wanted to become an actress and for the years of her late teens until she was thirty she was a failed actress playing tiny parts , understudying two or three tiny parts, getting the sack every few weeks, living in the cheapest lodgings and this book was a detailed account of these persistent failures- never the smallest success. There was no word of her plays and her success in later life. It was quite amusing in parts and she kept her sense of humour, but I was wanting to hear about the writing of her plays!

Rosemary bought from the ten pence sale of books a book by Ann Haydon Jones*, (she went in the afternoon so only paid five pence) the bits about King's Norton, King's Heath in Birmingham and The Priory were of interest but the book is pretty deadly otherwise; I have just glanced through it and it's mostly an account of who she beat or who beat her at table-tennis or tennis- your letters are much better.

58

Are you watching "Jane Eyre" on the television? I think that it is good but we will miss three weeks of it. I looked forward to Jane Austen's "Mansfield Park" but was disappointed. It was just bits and pieces of the book.

Much Love, Mother and Dad

*Rosemary had been at King's Norton Grammar School in Birmingham with Ann Haydon Jones

My Dears,

There is no doubt that I enjoyed every minute of my stay with you – it is as good as a tonic and I come back quite refreshed. The journey home was easy and pleasant. I did the Daily Telegraph crossword and helped a young man with the easy one (which I couldn't finish) I do not like those crosswords and the chap did not do much of it either, he wasn't very bright in any way. He let a much older woman help a very old man with his suitcase without batting an eyelash. A family of a mother and her three teenage daughters travelled from Bath to Salisbury with lots of plastic bags of pleasant-looking shopping. They were all lovely, large but not fat. The youngest was about Tessa's age, full faced and absolutely beautiful, the other two not quite so lovely. The middle one knocked over her carton of juice and spilled some on the floor. The mother smiled and gave her some tissues to wipe it up. I said " British Rail will never have been so clean". The girl wiped her shoe and the incident was over. A delightful quartet. My train arrived bang on time.

I have just found an apt quotation from Byron whom I know nothing about and it is from his "Don Juan" which I have not read

"The English winter –
ending in July

To recommence in August"

It is true this year except for a pleasant lapse in July.

How about this for a delightful story? I believe that I told you that the congregation had prayed for some help with the boys' and girls' brigade and help appeared for both groups. Rosemary asked a small boy to

F.AO: PHILLIP'S, DAD
SENDER: GOD

write about it for the church news-letter and he wrote "God got the message and passed it on to Philip's Dad". Isn't it delightful?

Much Love,
Mother and Dad

My Dears,

It's a beautiful day here today, cloudless blue sky, sunshine and no wind and I am not feeling at all workish. I suppose I could find something to clean if I looked hard enough but I am not keen so I am not looking; in fact I have just

spent the last half hour reading the newspaper. I watched the rugby match on Saturday which I greatly enjoyed – it was really exciting so I had to read all about that and then on the back page of the Sporting Extra there was a picture of the champion cross-country schoolboy runner who was from the Judd School (Tom and Colin's school). It is a good picture as there is a herd of deer crossing right across the stream of runners. The Judd boy had passed on his own before the deer interfered with the runners and all the rest had to wait for the deer to pass or get mixed up with them!

The real reason for this letter is to thank you for your lovely visit last weekend. It was lovely of you to come and I enjoyed your company so much. I hope that the long drive home was not too tiring.

I have a few snowdrops out in the garden but they are not very good ones and there are some crocus blooming too but they are also second-rate. I am hoping that some finer specimens will emerge later to prove that spring is truly here.

I am well through my Oscar Wilde book and have just come to the unpleasant parts and they really are unpleasant, truly foul. Whilst reading the chapters referring to his four plays which were so successful, I was able to get out my little book of the four and re-read them. They included, of course The Importance of Being Earnest, and although I've seen it quite four times I enjoyed reading it again. It is a masterpiece of its kind. The other three are very dated and sentimental - he lays it on very thickly.

It was kind of you to write when you heard of Nancy's* death. I was a bit shattered when I heard the news of her death but, strangely, the day of her funeral was a happy day. Nothing could take fifty three years of friendship away and I was so thankful that she had not had to suffer months of pain and helplessness. She had been ill, on and off for many years with kidney trouble but somehow managed to live a full and happy life. I got to Clapham easily and enjoyed the walk to Nancy's home along the edge of Clapham Common, all so familiar. Then I walked up Broomwood Rd and saw the flats for the elderly that had been built on the site of the Methodist Church where I belonged and first met Father. I then walked round to see the church hall, now converted into the church, before going to Nancy's home. It was a small gathering at the house and of the three women, one was named Rosemary and the other Ruth!!! All were very interesting people and my hearing-aid was doing its stuff so I was able to join in and hear the most interesting conversations which I greatly enjoyed. After the ceremony at the cemetery we had a delicious lunch which John, Nancy's brother, had prepared (by courtesy he said of Marks and Spencer) and I was home in Shoreham by five thirty. Father had bought some splendid cod so in twenty minutes or so a good meal was ready.

Splendid cod!

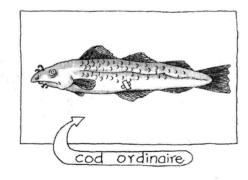

cod ordinaire

Here's a good tale that I was told the other day. A friend whose surname is Rudolph but who is known to everyone as Rudolph, had a much-loved cat called Micky who needed to be taken to the vet as it was unwell. The receptionist said "Name please" and he said "Rudolph" and she answered "Oh! That's a nice name for a cat". The next time he went he was prepared so when asked "Name please" he said "Micky " and the receptionist said "No, I want your surname not your first name."

We had a splendid Women's Fellowship on Wednesday. Our organist who has recently retired gave us a talk on church organs. He gave a very brief history and brought along six pipes of different sizes and was able to demonstrate the sounds by blowing into them. He had brought tapes and played short excerpts of organs from the earliest to the latest including one of Schweitzer. It really was a fascinating afternoon and he decorated his talk with plenty of funny stories. It was quite a treat.

I had yet another flood in the kitchen. I left the cold tap on full, whilst filling the washing machine, to answer the telephone and when I returned had to swim from the kitchen door to the washer (Butterfly Stroke). When it was all mopped up I sank, fortunately landing in an easy chair in the other room.

I am reading my new book Bernard Levin's "Enthusiasms" and have greatly enjoyed it but thought that he went too much over the top about opera. I know that he is crackers about opera and also very knowledgeable but there is no need to get **so** excited. Mind you, he did warn us in the title of his book and I am all for being enthusiastic, but there is reason in all things.

This last bit has been written whilst the meat and two veg have been cooking for our expected lunch guests, one of whom is a vegetarian. I am sprinkling grated cheese over the veg!! How is that for originality?

Lots of love to you all,
Mother and Dad

*Nancy was a very old and dear friend from the time Mother lived in Clapham Common before she was married

My Dears,

As Tess hopes for a tortoise I thought that she might like the enclosed-"A Book of Prayers From the Ark" which I find utterly delightful, the butterfly prayer seems to fly hither and thither, hardly resting a moment, the giraffe feeling very superior with his head very near the Heaven etc. I enjoy reading them over and over again.

I had a lovely time with Susie in Aberystwyth and with with Doug* in Birmingham but the train journey home from Birmingham was an adventure. At Birmingham New Street Station I was told that the train to Brighton was cancelled and that I had to change in London. I said "Oh No, Oh No" in a horrified voice as it meant that I would have to go from Euston to Victoria. There were thousands of steps down to the Victoria line and a few miles of corridors on top of that (or rather at the bottom of that). Anyway I arrived eventually in Brighton hoping to see Eric and after waiting half an hour I decided that it was time to try my hand at the public phone, an action that I avoid at all costs. I then discovered that Eric was at home waiting for me to call so had to wait twenty minutes for him. I amused myself looking at all the people on the station - every person under twenty five was wearing jeans-interesting. All the family were mad with me that I went on the underground instead of using a taxi. I MUST GET TAXI-MINDED.

Whilst I was away steps were the order of the day. I have never seen so many. Everywhere in Aberystwyth had its flight of stairs, - my hotel, Susie's house and everywhere that we visited had stairs, stairs and stairs. Then in Birmingham with Doug we went for a glorious walk in a wooded valley that finished with the longest and steepest flight of woodland stairs that I have ever seen and certainly ever climbed.

I have just been to the optician to see about new glasses as I do not like the ones I have. A very pleasant young woman examined my eyes very thoroughly and told me that there was nothing wrong with my eyes and that my sight was remarkable for one of my ancient years. (She didn't exactly put it like that!)

I came out walking on air for my eyes are so precious to me.

I have been making yet more cards and one is for Jonathan's birthday which was a yell. I drew tiny Eights** and when I had finished could see that the cox was directing them in one direction and they were all rowing in the opposite way or appeared to be, so I altered the figures and it looked better. They were not really figures but just blobs!

I have got into the habit lately of putting lots of bits of information in brackets - I can't make up my mind whether it's a bad thing or classy - probably the former. What do you think?

Your ever loving, Mother

*Mother's brother
**Jonathan rowed whilst at Oxford

My Dears,

It's a cold, wet, dirty dangerous way (in the words of Tony Lumpkin) if one ventures out but here I am, snug as a bug in a rug with time to write to you. I've already wasted half the time at my disposal doing the crossword. Thank you for your lovely letter and no, I do not like the envelopes either, but are MORE than ready to receive them because of the contents. Use them up until the stock is exhausted.

I saw "Pride and Prejudice" for the second time on the television and enjoyed it more. I think the on the first showing my anticipation was so great, nothing would have come up to its standard so I was glad to see it once again in a more reasonable mood. Mr. Bennett was perfect and Mr. Collins very good but Mrs. Bennett was far too loud. I see her as a stupid woman totally unaware that her remarks are upsetting everyone, especially Mr B. I am sure that she wouldn't have spoken in such a loud penetrating voice as after all they dined out with at least six families. I think Darcy and Bingley couldn't be better but I am still disappointed with Jane and Elizabeth. Jane isn't beautiful at all and Elizabeth hasn't that natural charm which has no need of being aware of it. I am sure that the Bennett's house is far too grand, there was a picture of it in the Daily Telegraph and it was a stately home which the Bennett's house certainly wasn't and there was also a picture of "Rosings" which wasn't any grander. Not much anyhow!

Thank you for "Pemberley". I was really glad to have it and read it but I HATED IT. I have never been so mad with a book in all my long life. It was quite an experience. The author just used every character in Pride and Prejudice in the dullest possible way and in the most common-or-garden English. By the middle of the book I was blazing with anger and my hair was

standing on end. I feel that she has no right to make use of these characters from one of the most beautiful and beloved books ever written. (I'm not partial am I?) After I had cooled down somewhat I started on the second half of the book-Well!!! It was unbelievable. Elizabeth moaning and whining because she didn't have a baby as soon as she was married, as if Eliza would behave like that, and then her stupidity in claiming that this unknown French woman's child was Darcy's and after all that to land the child at the noble Bingley's door. I do not think that Barbara Cartland could have done better. Then the final touch, Elizabeth was pregnant. Well, well, the book was quite a new experience for me.

Many thanks,
All my love Mother

My Dears

I had a treat this week when we went to the Community Centre to see "Twelfth Night". I had been hoping to go as the amateur company is usually first-rate and have a good productions. Malvolio was superb and Viola charming but her supposedly lookalike brother Sebastian was hopeless. A head taller than Viola and nothing like her to look at so that aspect of the play was a dead loss. Sir Andrew Aguecheek was very good but Sir Toby was too handsome a man for the part but did his best to overcome his flashing good looks! Feste was good but miscast, he should be slender and not middle-aged. Olivia was delightful but Orsino was hopeless. His voice when he opened the play with that beautiful speech "If music be the food of love, play on" was ghastly. Still I know the play almost backwards and enjoyed the evening.

This letter, as you can see, comes on very superior notepaper which I found in the bureau, I cannot trace its history but fancy it may be a cut off from some important information. It will be enclosed in an envelope which has not been used more than once before but I am sure that you are not fussy as long as you receive a letter.

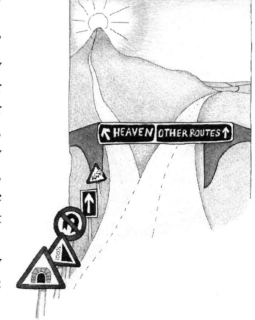

I have just read "Much Ado About Nothing" again as it is such a good tale . I have only just finished the book Jonathan gave me for my birthday entitled "Is Shakespeare our Contemporary" The first chapter was a corker, heavy going to say the least but to my great joy the next chapter and the next were marvellous, fascinating, and so it was until the last-but-one chapter which wasn't my cup of tea. The last chapter blossomed again. I really enjoyed it.

Two short stories; Susie, when she was very young on seeing her first funeral drive by said: " Are they driving him to heaven?"

Richard also very young on going to a cemetery said "What's that?" so was told and he said "Do they put them in the coffins or do they climb in?"

All My Love, Mother

My Dears,

Glorious sunshine is pouring into my room.

I wrote that much and then a friend arrived to see me. She is a friend from church and has been very kind since Father died and comes here each week if possible and we spend a pleasant time together. We haven't much in common, well nothing really, not like my friend Eva, who comes for an evening once a week when we have fabulous discussions as she is bright and very knowledgeable and stirs up my poor brains. My friend stayed until lunch time and it is now two o'clock and I had planned to get this letter into the post this morning but here I am with hardly anything written. It is quite a time since I have written but you are so busy that I feel a letter is better than a phone call.

I am sorry that you had a dull Court session this week* You had no sooner sent that chap to prison for not paying his poll-tax then the government announced that non-poll-tax payers could claim compensation if they are sent to prison, but I expect that was for people who literally had no money to pay rather than those who defied the law.

We had our Church Annual General Meeting on Sunday after the service and quite a crowd stayed. I plucked up courage to speak as the BBC are dramatizing the novel "The Buccaneers" by Edith Wharton. Because Edith Wharton died before the novel as completed, the BBC finished it by adding a rape-scene and a homosexual bedroom-scene. An American has written objecting so I felt that it was time we **did** something and not just say "Oh Dear". I asked for permission to write to the BBC on behalf of our minister and the congregation to let them know in no uncertain terms that we objected to such a degrading ending to a good book. I wrote to the script writer Maggie Wadey who has argued that if a book is unfinished you are justified in ending it any way you like. I think that is crazy logic. I received an enthusiastic response to my request. I do not like to speak as my voice can go husky quite without warning and, as I will record in a moment, I am adept at falling flat on my face, anyhow I do not like seeing aged people performing when there are younger ones to

71

do it. It's like church organists who will not give up their posts and leave their beloved organs even though they cannot hit the right notes.

The squirrels have eaten all the bulbs that I planted in the pots on my veranda, daffs, crocus, snowdrops and hyacinths all gone. I hope that they enjoyed them as I am now deprived of a colourful show.

There was a marvellous half-page article in the Daily Telegraph recently from a former headmistress on the teaching of reading** and I was so impressed that I wrote to her and had a reply that I found most attractive, to the point and sufficient. It was on beautifully headed notepaper and read (I had addressed her as Irina Tyk as I did not know if she was a Mrs. or a Miss and she addressed me in the same manner)

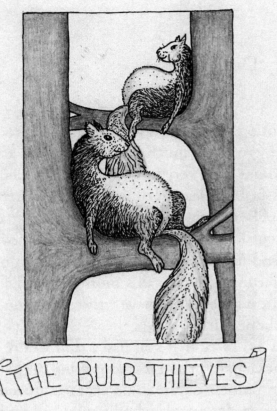

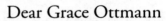
THE BULB THIEVES

Dear Grace Ottmann
"The Daily Telegraph 24.5.95"
Your support and encouragement are greatly appreciated.
I thank you.
Yours sincerely,
Irina Tyk

I thought it concise (it certainly was that!) but sufficient and sincere. What do you think? I also sent the article to Mollie Walsh who taught the class who left me, (mine were the five to six year olds and hers were the six to seven year olds) and she was a brilliant teacher. I have had no contact for years save the annual Christmas card but after receiving the article she wrote to me a long, marvellous letter which I greatly enjoyed receiving. Molly will be ninety next birthday and still writes a beautiful hand. I was amazed to have her letter.

Now I must record my amazing evening last Monday. At tea one of my teeth fell out when I got up. I lost my balance and fell flat on the carpet, mercifully avoiding any of the furniture – the advantages of a spacious room. When cleaning my teeth later I discovered it was not one of my teeth that had come out but an isolated one from my plate and it had also taken off a chunk of the plate. Next morning I rang the dentist who luckily had an appointment at ten past ten so I went and took the bits and pieces with me and gave them to the dentist who said he could mend it by mid-day. Hopefully Rosemary will be able to fetch it and bring it to me. I feel half dressed without it even though it is a small plate.

It is such a beautiful day that it will be a pleasure to walk to the post box to post this to you.

All my love,
Mother

*Ruth is a local JP
**Grace was a primary school teacher who ensured that all her pupils left her class aged 6 able to read

My Dears,

Your letters and phone calls, phone calls and letters strew my path and have been more welcome than I can express. I have been inordinately lazy and not feeling like doing anything. I spent the morning sitting in the chair doing nothing but feel somewhat livelier this afternoon. I've written you several letters in my head, fine, well expressed letters too, but they came to nothing.

Did you like Swansea Brian? I once stayed at the university in my student days for a Welsh Council Committee for the Student Christian Movement. The men used to come into breakfast with wet shoes to pretend that they had been out walking (great fun) but we were young and innocent in those days.

Thank you for the Shakespeare crossword. I glanced down the clues and couldn't see one that jumped to life but on a second reading managed ONE. Oh Dear. All the rest became more and more obscure and if I understood the clues they seemed to come chiefly from the histories, which are not my strong point and if they came from the plays I know I couldn't think of the names (which is common practice in daily life I am sad to say). My anticipation of a treat came to nothing to my great disappointment.

What do you think of this? Rosemary gave me Bernard Levin's book "Speaking Up" as an extra birthday gift which is a collection of his journalistic articles, chiefly from The Times, and one is called "Smoke Signals" which is about his grandfather who was a heavy smoker. His grandfather's preferred brand was Kensitas, which I seem to remember went in for a somewhat classier cigarette card than the other manufacturers. One was, Bernard Levin wrote, a spectacular set, not of cards, but of leaves of silk on which were produced the flags of the nations. Talk about co-incidences, I vaguely remember them from my youth but as we were a non-smoking lot, we saw very few, but how strange that I should read about them after just seeing your Mother's collection, Brian.

We had a spot of luck at the Women's fellowship this week. The speaker was an ex-headmaster who comes each year and is greatly enjoyed as he speaks very clearly. His subject this week was hymns written by Sussex writers and it was most interesting as he is such a fine speaker. When I knew in the morning his subject my heart sank because our pianist, though a delightful woman, is no great guns on the piano, in fact her left hand doth not know what her right hand doeth. Until a year ago we had a superb pianist but alas, she now lives in Broadstairs. About two-fifty who should walk into the Fellowship but Peggy, our erstwhile pianist. Our regular pianist has said that she would be thankful to stand down if we could find a better player so I knew she wouldn't mind relinquishing the piano stool. A good afternoon was had by all and the hymns sung to fine accompaniment.

Lots of love to you all, Mother

My Dears

This grotty foolscap is all the I have left, I did not realize that I was at the end of my reserves so must replenish my stock. Your letter has just come, a most welcome sight on the porch shelf. My thankfulness sometimes overwhelms me when I think of my four families. What more can any Mother want or ask for, than four loving families sharing their lives with me in such marvellous ways.

Susie had an amazing report for her six weeks' work experience with schizophrenic patients saying that she was the best student that they had had. When the document was signed and sealed she went to post it and before it reached the letterbox the wind blew it out of her hand into the middle of the road. After the wheels of a bus had run over it she was able to rescue it but it was filthy and torn so she sent it into the college with an explanation and said that she would endeavour to get a replacement. What a yell.

Are you thinking of sending me a birthday present????????????? What I would like is another Elizabeth Gaskell (a paperback will do). I have this HUGE hardback of her life and I am quite happy with paperbacks of her novels. I only have "Mary Barton" and "North and South". I have read "Ruth" and "Cranford" years ago but do not have copies of them. "Wives and Daughters" would be good as I have not read it. I am planning to read the novel when I come to it in the biography written by Jenny Uglow. I did this when I read the biography of Oscar Wilde and enjoyed that.

Sorry about this brief letter. I read that Mrs Gaskell liked to sit and answer letters that she had just received and I always want to do the same. You never know I might become famous in an after-life. I have no time to become famous on this earth. I am about one third the way through Jenny Uglow's biography and the amount of knowledge that she has amazes me. I don't know how one person can know so much.

Lots of love to all,

Mother

My Dears,

Two letters from you, Ruth, and one from Tess in three days. I am rich indeed.

There is no sign of my ear apparAHtus (Emphasis the AH, it sounds more classy) so I am in the process of getting another. Rosemary took me to Worthing Hospital, a vast place, but such a nice young woman measured me up. It will take two to three weeks to arrive and then it will mean another jaunt to Worthing. The sun is making a valiant effort to shine and I think that it will succeed. Let's hope so. I bought a 1901 diary, no, a 2001 diary, and it's a horrid one, so I am going to buy another. I cannot bear the thought of using this one for a whole year.

I have just read Shakespeare's "Antony and Cleopatra", I must have seen it as I knew the story but I do not think that I have read it before, although some of the quotes are very famous. Sadly, some of it was unintelligible to my dull mind- what does this mean- "High-battled Caesar will unstate his happiness and be stag'd to the short against a sworder! I see men's judgements are a parcel of their fortunes and things outward do draw the inward quality after them to suffer all alike that he should dream. Knowing all measures, the full Caesar will answer his emptiness" I don't believe it!!!!!

Answers and clues will wing their way to you in next weeks' missive. There are scores of paragraphs as obscure as this, at least to me.

How lovely that I am to come and stay with you and that you will fetch me, old age has its compensations. You have a book or two that I can browse through when you are busy. The world seems to have gone mad over Oscar Wilde. Funnily enough I bought "The Reading Gaol" poem which is tragic piece but very moving and then I bought a paperback of "The Picture of Dorian Grey" which I didn't enjoy at all until it came to the end, when it was brilliant writing. Then out of the blue someone gave me the complete works of Wilde so I have read his four most popular plays. As I have seen "The Importance of Being Earnest" so often I decided I wouldn't read it but I couldn't resist, as it is such a delight. It so totally lacks any serious content that I am sure that it will be popular for ever.

I am writing this on my knee in front of the FIRE. Is mid-June and it reminds me of the holiday one June that Dad and I had in Scarborough when we nearly froze. It rained solidly and we had a trip to the Yorkshire Moors and saw nothing but mist and rain. We visited Flamborough Head but couldn't see it only hearing the foghorns. It was no more like June than it is today so we must try and recall last week or last year when we sweltered watching them play tennis on the Centre Court.

All my love, Mother

My Dears

A lovely morning though a bit chilly. I took the opportunity of washing a sheet and some towels and they are all out in the sunshine and the wind.

To say I was glad to have your letter, Ruth, is putting it mildly. You rang early on Monday to tell me to listen to "Paradise Lost" on Radio Four but you obviously over-estimated my grey matter. On Monday I had a check-up with the doctor and I did some shopping so when I returned Milton was off the air. On Tuesday some friends came for coffee so poor old Milton had the cold shoulder. On Wednesday I started to listen and after a while I was none the wiser, got no pleasure from the poetry so switched it off in the middle of the broadcast. If I had heard the first one there might have been some explanation and guidance by some learned gentleman that would have helped me but being plunged into the middle of the epic and into the end at that, I climbed out to save myself from drowning.

To continue about your letter Ruth or rather lack of it. When nothing came by Saturday I could stand it no longer so rang and had a lovely long chat to you, Brian, so looked forward to your letter on Monday - nothing - Tuesday, nothing - Wednesday, nothing. By this time I was desperate but I knew all was well as Brian had told me so. Then Thursday came and with it you're most welcome letter. I LOVE your letters and do not ever recall such a sterile gap. Many, many thanks for all your loving letters. You wrote "It seems ages since I wrote" and in return I quote my dear friend Hamlet. "Seems, Madam! Nay it is, I know not seems" Yes, I saw and much enjoyed the David Attenborough programme and have also watched the Peter Cooke and Dudley Moore programme in memory of Peter Cooke. I do not think that I have ever seen their programmes so thought that I should see possibly the last that will be shown and I found it very, very funny, so I was glad that I had watched it.

In the West Sussex Gazette, which I take instead of the local paper and the deadly Methodist Recorder, there is a lovely, quite large picture of four lady artists. One is of Juliet Pannet, the mother of the artist who painted my Dorset painting. Another is of Paula Thrift who painted my rose picture so I was very interested in the article. Three of them are holding pictures which they have painted. Paula Thrift's are one of flowers and Juliet Pannet's a street scene which looks very good. She actually specializes in drawing the heads of famous people and they are superb. In my art book by Edward Wesson there is a drawing of him by Juliet Pannet which I greatly admire.

I have just finished a book on the home life in Birmingham's worst slums in Hockley in the early years of this century* and the poverty and privation was unbelievable. The school had to provide some breakfast and had an annual handout of clothes, shoes and blankets. When I taught in the Old Kent Road in London in the Thirties the poorest children had to be given shoes. Times have changed some what thank goodness.

It was good to see Jonathan and we had a very happy evening when he took three of us out for a meal. I enjoyed the company more than the meal as the vegetables (carrots and cauliflower) were as hard as bullets. I do not think they had

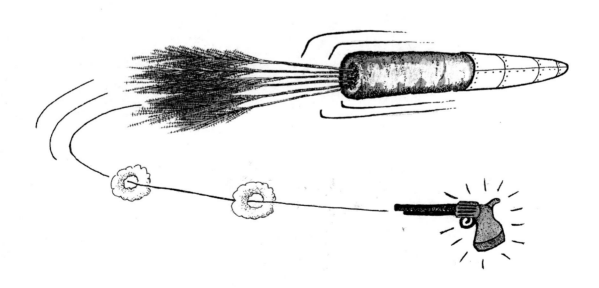

been actually shown the hot water. I know that it is the modern way of cooking vegetables but I do not like it. Anyhow we had a good cup of coffee and the others enjoyed the meal.

You must be beginning rehearsals soon for the university musical - here's to success, it must be fun and I know that the students will love it. I know I loved anything on stage when I was young, whether it was the dramatics at school, college, at the Church in London or sitting in the gods at the Old Vic's every production.

Now I must go and find an envelope. Oh, I have a new inside to my gold watch which now has a battery so I do not have to wind it up and it's always telling me the correct time. This is such a change as it never told me the right time before.
Now to go to the post-box.

Your ever loving, Mother

*Grace lived in Birmingham from the late thirties until the sixties

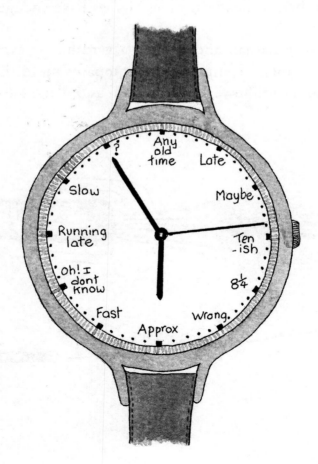

My Dears,

I warn you, Ruth, I'm not in the letter-writing mood so what follows probably will not be worth reading but you never can tell as the mood may lighten as my biro gets to work.

The warmth of your visit is still with me, I loved every minute of it. You know that my hands have been covered in a rash that has nearly sent me mad. The ointment from the doctor did no good at all and then yesterday I had a visitor who said 'Do you think that it could be this plant?' so when she arrived back at her home she looked in some book that she had and there was a picture of the very plant and the wording said 'This primula is the ONLY primula that can cause a rash' and I realized that I had had the rash for the two-and-a-half weeks that I had the plant. As I had a second appointment with the doctor I kept it. I told him of my discovery and he was very interested. I wrapped the plant up in wads of newspaper and in hours there was an improvement. In two days the rash had gone completely just leaving my hands a bit pink but with no discomfort. Quite amazing. I will not buy a plant like that again in a hurry.

Did I tell you that I have had two books that I treasure returned to me THREE years after lending them to one of Susie's friends! I had mentioned it to the girl's mother who found them happily sitting on her daughter's bookshelves. One was A. L. Rowse's book on Shakespeare, which is fabulous. The Mother knew they were mine as my name was inscribed in them so they were returned to me and I have enjoyed dipping into them once again.

It's a pity that John Major hasn't got a better team to assist him; the Foreign Secretary seems his only strong one. As for the farmer's chap, he's a dead loss, I'm sure he wouldn't know a cow from a sheep!

I'll stop now as I feel that I am wasting your time making you read this inconsequential letter, but it comes with much love.

Mother

My Dears,

It is Monday morning and I have been messing around taking all morning to do simple tasks. I have done a great deal of writing of late of the ornamental kind so this is why you have not received a letter for a day or two. I have drawn a cover for Susie's school kitchen project, a card for the minister's fiftieth birthday and now someone wants a card for a diamond wedding and even though I asked you on the telephone for a bright idea of some suitable words none has been forthcoming. "Diamonds are a girl's best friend" "Diamonds are forever" and "Like a diamond in the sky" are the sum total of suggestions from my buddies which do not inspire me. The other writing that I have been doing is the Kipling poem that is to be framed and hung in his garden at Rottingdean. My calligraphy teacher is being so helpful and making lovely suggestions but it is a big task for me as the poem is quite long and I am fearful of making a mistake. I am practising the script and illustrations on ordinary paper before I start using the expensive paper.

I have TWO bowlfuls of flowers from the huge bouquet of flowers that you sent courtesy of Mr. M&S for my birthday; the white tulips are beautiful and look like this and not like this the usual manner of tulips. Thank you so much. I have had masses of lovely cards, numerous bunches of flowers and TEN packets of notelets (People seem to know that I write the odd letter or two). Most of them inclined to be of the botanical nature, I will reserve them for my more intelligent correspondents. I do not mean to imply anything by that statement of course. One is not ninety for nothing, though its uses are not always apparent. Thank you too for the beautiful card, the artist, according to the blurb on the back was quite famous. Many cards this day are well worth sending and receiving and give a great deal of pleasure. I'm glad that your latest production was a great success, a good amateur performance is so exiting for the performers and this carries over the footlights and everyone is happy.

The garden looks lovely, there are masses of lovely daffs and the pansies are in bloom and the flowers in the troughs are colourful. The winter jasmine has been a picture though it is now turning into leaf mode.

I had a good letter from Jonathan and when I had read it for the third time I decided to chuck it so tore it up. Within minutes I was reading your letter saying that you only get the shortest notes and phone calls and I decided that you would have enjoyed his letter to me! I then fetched the sellotape and began sticking it all together again, so I am sending it to you in its remodelled state which you can throw away when you have read it. I hope that you enjoy it as it took me AGES to repair together with masses of patience with the almost uncontrollable sellotape.

All my love, Mother

My Dear Ones,

The hairdresser was due today but she is ill so I had ample time to enjoy your letter and am inspired to answer it straightaway.

I hope that you have been able to cast the next musical at the university successfully. I really laughed about the student who said that she could make all the rehearsals but wasn't certain about the performances! I am reminded of the performances of my youth and how I loved them. I know the students will recall their involvement with great pleasure in the years to come. They certainly were highlights for me.

Our beautiful willow tree is ruined. It would sway gracefully in the wind but last week the gales were too much for it and a great bough snapped off and is over the lawn. A tree expert said that the main trunk could be saved but a beautiful bough that has split from the main trunk must go. It was such a beautiful tree that I am greatly saddened. Another flowering tree near my window has to go too as its roots were damaging the pond which has goldfish. Anybody can have the fish and the pond if the tree can stay but, alas, the goldfish won.

Now I know all about faxes. You push a letter in a slot in your sitting room and it comes out in India or any other outpost. I do not like the slur of being ignorant, so do not presume any more that I am not up to date with technowlegy (not too certain about spelling though).

I have just re-read 'The Winter's Tale' and now it is clear in my mind. There is some beautiful verse in the second half,
'Daffodils that come before the swallows dare
And take the winds of March with beauty'
What language. I shall love to come to Bristol again and to see "A Midsummer Night's Dream" would be wonderful. I know chunks of it by heart." Chunks" is such an ugly word to refer to "hanging a pearl in every cowslip's ear" but the humour of Bottom and his crowd is a never-ending delight.

Did you see the notice of the death of Leslie French? He was my delight when I was young, a superb Puck and Ariel. He was a dancer as well as an actor of the first class and it is his and Gielgud's figures sculpted on the front of the BBC building as Puck and Oberon.

There was a fantastic dawn this morning, crimson stripes right across the heavens. With my three windows I see all that goes on in the sky, it is marvellous.

All my love, Mother

To you all with love,

A very happy birthday Ruth. I expect that you will celebrate somehow. It might mean an extra sausage for tea. Thank you for your most interesting letter, words fail me, I mean that literally (Is that how you spell it but I am too lazy to fetch the dictionary so you will have to guess what I mean) Forgive my accustomed foolscap but I do like lines to write along.

The outside of the Burrell Collection gives no idea of the beauties within, as I thought it plain and uninteresting and almost ugly to house such beauty but inside I loved the tall slender windows looking out onto the green grass. I seem to remember that the donor of the building wanted to build in a beautiful landscape so had to go outside Glasgow. I cannot remember many details of what we saw but recall some wonderful china.

Thank you for the postcard of "Romeo and Juliet" from Stratford but I didn't really like it. Juliet looks older than a teenager should look and I thought looked rather bewildered as if she couldn't fathom what it was all about. Romeo, I liked the look of him, but from the photograph couldn't really know what he was thinking or feeling.

The "Merchant" sounded fabulous - what a brilliant idea to make one of the suitors a very old man and be gloriously funny to relieve a play with little or no humour in it.

Did you say "Would I like another trip to Stratford?" Would I???? It is the Red Letter day of the year for me even if it rains all day. I try hard not to be envious of your visits as it is foolish to envy and when we lived in Birmingham I paid many visits to the theatre. I realize that I am extremely fortunate to be able to see a play at all in my extreme old age so thank you for the marvellous privilege.

I am reading Jane Austen's "Northanger Abbey" again. It is a silly story, really not in the same league as "Pride and Prejudice" or "Emma" but it does show the futility of women's lives compared with today. I am glad that I did not live then. It has a great deal about Bath which is interesting.

I have been given four books, your lovely poetry book and another poetry book from Rosemary with poems from the Middle Ages to the present day all about Jesus as teacher, healer, and his birth and resurrection. I would have to live another ninety years to devour them all but I can pick and choose. My other two are a yell. They are from Richard, Susie and Sally and they have been obviously chosen by Sally. One is so heavy that I can hardly hold it and is entitled "Lives of the Poets" The print is so small it is almost impossible to read and it will not fit on my shelves! It will be earmarked for Sally in the future handout. The other one is almost as big and heavy and is by an American Shakespearean scholar and is a masterpiece with his knowledge of the thirty-seven plays and poems. Anyway, struggling to hold the volume on my lap I have read most of what he says about "The Dream" and "Twelfth Night" with the help of a magnifying glass and enjoyed a great deal of what I read. What I couldn't understand I just skipped. As you can understand I will not be reading what he says about "Timon of Athens", "Pericles" or "Cymbeline"

Now I will go and post this, the sun is shining and I can catch the two-thirty clearance.

My love to you, Mother

ACKNOWLEDGMENTS

Cathy Snowden for her delightful illustrations

Sally Bayley for her thoughtful contribution

Brian, my husband, for his support in this venture

Elinor Edwards for her help and advice

SALLY BAYLEY

Sally Bayley is Teaching and Research Fellow at the Rothermere American Institute, University of Oxford. She is the author of "Eye Rhymes": Sylvia Plath's Art of the Visual (OUP, 2007), the first book to present Plath's large body of paintings and drawings to the public. The book was reviewed on Woman's Hour, The Sunday Times and Oprah Winfrey's magazine "O" and featured in an arts evening at the South Bank Centre.

She is also author of "Representing Sylvia Plath" (CUP 2011), an interdisciplinary study of Plath's several afterlives in the realm of popular culture, psychology, photography, art and film. In 2010 she completed a study of the American home in literature, art, film and popular culture, "Home on the Horizon": America's Search for Space, from Emily Dickinson to Bob Dylan (Peter Lang, 2010). She has recently completed a more popular book of non fiction on the diary as a form of writing and self-recording, Diaries: from "Pepys to Tweets". She is currently completing a childhood memoir.

CATHY SNOWDEN

'In the 70's I trained as a potter at West Surrey College of Art and Design. I subsequently set up a pottery in central Bristol and specialised in domestic tableware. When I looked up from my wheel and out through my window, I had a glorious view of three weathercocks catching the sun, and slowly revolving atop the spires of nearby churches.

Later, I ran general art workshops from my studio at home. It is situated at the bottom of my garden and is surrounded by trees, fields and curious cows. Students' dogs attended too, and enjoyed a game of ball when we stopped for a coffee break!

I have long been interested in constructing and decorating objects made of papier mâché. These are embellished with intricately painted patterns or scenes. From a decorative perspective, I was intrigued when Ruth asked me if I would consider illustrating her mother's letters; they have been a rich and varied source of comic inspiration and have been an absolute joy to work on.

I live in South Gloucestershire with my husband, a dog, and three querulous lovebirds. I currently work full-time at a nearby castle, co-running a beautiful tropical butterfly house.'